W9-DIU-990

Teacher to Teacher

A GUIDEBOOK FOR EFFECTIVE MENTORING

JANE FRASER

HEINEMANN
Portsmouth, NH

To learners of all ages

Heinemann
A division of Reed Elsevier Inc.
361 Hanover Street
Portsmouth, NH 03801–3912
http://www.heinemann.com

Offices and agents throughout the world

© 1998 by Jane Fraser

All rights reserved. No part of this book may be reproduced in any form or by any electronic or mechanical means, including information storage and retrieval systems, without permission in writing from the publisher, except by a reviewer, who may quote brief passages in a review.

Library of Congress Cataloging-in-Publication Data

Fraser, Jane.
    Teacher to Teacher : a guidebook for effective mentoring / Jane Fraser.
       p.   cm.
    Includes bibliographical references and index.
    ISBN 0-325-00012-3
    1. Mentoring in education—United States. 2. Teachers—United States. 3. Interpersonal relations—United States. I. Title
    LB1731.4.F73   1998
    371.102—dc21
                                         98-34287
                                         CIP

Editor: Lois Bridges
Production: Abigail M. Heim
Cover design: Darci Mehall, Aureo Designs
Cover photograph: Sarah Merriman
Manufacturing: Courtney Ordway

Printed in the United States of America on acid-free paper
02 01 00   DA   5

Contents

iii

Acknowledgments

BECAUSE THIS BOOK IS ABOUT THE EXPERIENCE OF BEING A mentor, it seems appropriate to mention some of my mentors, whose ideas and work stand behind this text. From them I learned priceless things that help my work. My mentors also taught me about life beyond teaching.

In Westport, Connecticut I have had the good fortune to teach and learn alongside the finest. I want to thank Caltha Crowe, Anne Nesbitt, and Donna Skolnick at Coleytown School, who are incredible, generous mentors and partners in learning. I also want to acknowledge Dana Barsi, Sheila Florio, Cathryn Kibby, Sarah Merriman, Enia Noonan, and Hilda Rhodes. Reaching back through the years, I want to thank Marian Bailey, Pat Beasley, JoAnn Davidson, and Mary Lou Woodruff for being friends and role models.

I learn as much from the new teachers in Westport as they learn from me. It is a privilege to know them in my role as retired teacher mentor. The two-way street will be evident from some of the stories in this book. I am deeply indebted to Tracie DeLawrence, Rob Grin, Whitney McCarthy, Ashley Moran, Kate Sanderson, Mara Schwartz, Linda Sweeney, Pam Syndercombe, Lesa Tischler, Karen Toth, and Karen Wrobel.

At The Reading and Writing Project important mentors have included Lucy Calkins, Randy Bomer, and the many learners in the Thursday afternoon group. Knowing these teachers and meeting with them regularly has been a unique privilege.

I want to express deep gratitude to my husband, Julius, my writing role model. He lighted my way while providing the needed support. I am grateful also to my daughters, Ann and Carol. In the beginning I was their mentor, but later I discovered how much there was to learn from them.

A special thanks goes to Lois Bridges, my Heinemann editor. Our E-mail talk has been intense as she contributed her expertise and thoughtful comments to this manuscript. I want to mention Donna Skolnick again. She was my first reader and a valued critic who nudged my thinking about this book as we met to talk about teaching and writing.

These mentors encouraged me to learn and to stretch my thinking. It is an exciting journey.

Introduction

In the opening scenes of "Mr. Holland's Opus" when Mr. Holland walked through the halls of his new school, his administrator told him that teaching was not "a fall-back position." Nor, as the movie unfolds, do we see the administration giving him meaningful support or assistance. Mr. Holland remarks, early on, that "this is going to be a lot rougher gig than I thought."

It is a rough gig, for beginning teachers especially, from learning to be good observers of students, implementing curriculum, understanding how children learn, being the cheerleader and the coach, and learning the culture of the school through work with parents and administrators. Teaching is no easy street on which we glide, roller blades in place, toward a fast-approaching summer vacation. It's not like that.

This book is about the growth and change that can be achieved by teachers, new and experienced, when they work together. Teachers helping protégés to learn is a rather recent idea. There are many models that could be cited, but I will talk about those I know best. My own state, Connecticut, has a formal program for mentors in the school building to assist beginning teachers as they adapt to their new profession. The Reading and Writing Project at Teachers College, led by Lucy Calkins, is committed to bringing about change through staff development in New York City and suburban districts.

This book draws on many years of teaching experience. Some of my stories come from my own classroom, peer coaching experiences, and staff development work in the Westport, Connecticut, Public Schools. My present work is with The Reading and Writing Project at Teachers College, Columbia University in city and suburban districts and as a mentor to teachers new to Westport. I draw upon notebooks that have helped me think through my work as a mentor to many protégés.

1

My view of how a mentor can help a colleague grow has changed over the years. In the beginning, I thought introducing new materials, having conversations, and doing model lessons was enough. Now I know that teaching adults is not really different from teaching young children. Adults learn best when they are interested. They need opportunities to practice, time to integrate and modify new ideas to fit their belief systems, and occasions to talk things over with peers. To be an effective mentor, one needs to include these elements and tailor them to the individual protégé.

When this book was like a glimmer of light flying through my thoughts, my husband and I visited the San Diego Wild Animal Park. The gorilla troop was mesmerizing. A surrogate mother carried a baby around on her back while a second baby dutifully imitated an older male. Two young gorillas stroked each other lovingly as they rolled on the ground under the watchful eye of a curious youngster. It occurred to me that our ability to model and learn from each other is something we share with the animal world. From an early age we look up to our mentors: our parents, siblings, peers, and teachers.

When I became an educator in the 1960s, I was startled at how isolated I felt. Sharing was not the norm. Things were competitive and secretive in the school where I taught. I vividly remember asking another first grade teacher why she had a stack of composition books on her desk. Her sharp reply was, "None of your business." I felt like a bad little girl rebuked for being too curious.

Happily, in the 1980s, rays of hope began to shine through dreary classrooms throughout our country. We gathered our papers, opened our doors, and began to talk with each other. The impetus for change came in large part from the research published by Lucy Calkins, Donald Graves, Jane Hansen, and Nancie Atwell, and later by the many teacher practitioners who joined them.

A group of teachers in Westport, led by my coauthor Donna Skolnick of *On Their Way, Celebrating Second Graders as They Read and Write* (1994), did classroom research. We met to share ideas and learn from each other. This had a qualitative difference from the inservice workshops we had attended year after year. It was not a delivery of another person's precepts. It was the work of teachers with teachers as many of us discovered that we learned better with collegial support. It helped to hear how someone else asked a question or solved a problem. The learning felt different, and the outcomes were earth shaking for those of us experiencing them. The way we thought of our teaching was forever changed. We wanted to reach toward the stars.

We became mentors for each other. We recognized the power of looking to mentors as a way to grow. We knew we could help each other learn new skills and try new strategies to increase our teaching repertoires. We helped each other discover the excitement and joy of learning that would accompany us on our lifelong journey through our professional and private lives.

Ruth Sidney Charney, writing in *Teaching Children to Care*, says, "Teaching is an extension and projection of a person, not just transplanted skills or acquired methods. Every day we reveal ourselves—our manners of organizing, habits of dealing with frustration, entrenched patterns of thought and interest" (1992, p. 256). Even those protégés who are lucky enough to have a mentor with whom they develop communication and respect must, in the end, find their own way toward growth and change. Mentors cannot impose changes on protégés like a uniform to wear or a cookbook of recipes to follow. We can only hope that protégés will chart their own successful course toward variety and excitement in their classrooms. Each person has his own music to play with its infinite possibilities and varieties. The goal of a mentoring relationship is to show the pathway to that music, be it a concerto, a symphony, or a soulful jazz tune.

In this book, Chapters 1 and 2 are about how to establish a mentor/protégé relationship and get it moving. Chapter 3 contains suggestions for helping protégés with classroom management. In Chapters 4 and 5, I consider protégé learning and reflection. Chapter 6 contains thoughts about working with the parent community, and Chapter 7 has suggestions for how reading aloud can impact upon the reading and writing workshop. Chapter 8 is about my peer coaching experiences, another model of teachers working together.

Teaching is *not* an easy gig but it can be smoother with the input of a sympathetic peer—a mentor who is there to help a protégé through the rough spots. That's what this book is intended to do, to make suggestions about how to follow the music together as we are transported by the singing of Marilyn Horne or the playing of Wynton Marsalis.

REFERENCES

Charney, Ruth Sidney. 1992. *Teaching Children to Care, Management in the Responsive Classroom*. Greenfield, MA: Northeast Foundation for Children.

Fraser, Jane and Donna Skolnick. 1994. *On Their Way, Celebrating Second Graders as They Read and Write*. Portsmouth, NH: Heinemann.

1

Starting Off On the Right Foot

COLLEGIALITY, TRUST, AND SUPPORT

*B*ecause this has been a cold, wet spring, I didn't plant my peas at the usual time. I thought the seeds might rot. Instead, I waited until the end of March, yet, two weeks later, I didn't see any sign of green. However, salad greens are a different story. I sowed arugula a week after the peas, and already there are the two rows of faithful shoots poking through.

BEING A MENTOR CAN BE LIKE HAVING A GARDEN. CONDITIONS must be right for learning and growth to occur. One important condition is some basic rapport between mentor and protégé. The relationship will grow stronger if the partners feel a kinship as they work toward a common goal.

In his February 2, 1995 column in the Sunday *New York Times*, Albert Shanker wrote "Sink or Swim" about the initiation of beginning teachers.

> Almost every other profession has a better system of induction for new members than teaching. Most offer some kind of internship that provides lots of help from experienced colleagues and allows beginners to ease into accepting full responsibilities. If teaching is ever to be a profession in the sense that medicine and law are, beginning teachers need a chance to learn what constitutes good practice with the help of accomplished colleagues instead of being forced to figure everything out for themselves.

Shanker's words can be extended to include experienced teachers who want to reach toward new practices with the help of colleagues. In this chapter, I discuss the conditions needed to begin a successful mentoring experience with beginning or experienced staff members. I draw upon my staff development experience with The Reading and Writing Project and my work as a retired teacher mentor in Westport. Throughout this chapter and the entire book, I illustrate points with stories from my notebooks.

The Westport work deserves special explanation. Five years ago, as experienced teachers began to retire and new staff was employed, the district made the ground-breaking decision to hire, on an hourly basis, six to ten retired teachers who could serve as mentors to new staff. The turnover in teachers was dramatic and the district felt it was wise to tap into the knowledge and experience of some retirees. The program is unique. Retired teacher mentors have no restrictions. We are encouraged to help with almost anything, for example, setting up a new classroom, the problems of adapting to an unknown school and community, as well as assisting with individual students and with curriculum. We have no evaluative responsibilities, we don't talk with administrative staff about how new teachers are doing, and this confidentiality places us in a unique role.

CHOICE OF TEACHERS: WHERE TO PLANT SEEDS

Seed and plant catalogs come with maps that indicate planting zones because sticking plants and seeds in unfriendly territory doesn't work. Just as different plants grow in different environments, the relationship between a mentor and a protégé requires the right climate. I worked in Millie's Bronx, New York, classroom as a staff developer for The Writing Project. I associate Millie's story with the arugula in my garden because everything worked well to produce a bumper crop. The following is from my notebook:

> It is obvious that Millie is an experienced, thoughtful teacher. Her fifth grade classroom is a tight ship. Today I met thirty-two students from eight different countries, in addition to the United States: Albania, Cambodia, Italy, Jamaica, Mexico, Nigeria, Puerto Rico, and Vietnam.
>
> Millie asked to work with me when she heard there would a staff developer in her school. At our initial meeting, she inquired about a genre study of picture books. She wants her students to have the experience of writing their own picture books. It makes sense to respect her choice.
>
> Millie and I agree on how we will work together. I will introduce each picture book with a mini-lesson and leave the book with her to use in the interval between my visits. I will coach her for these mini-lessons if she feels the need, otherwise she will make her own decisions based upon her observations of student writing. I like how she takes responsibility. She wants our work to move forward at a pace that is appropriate for the class and

her own learning. She plans to have writing workshop periods as often as she can to inspire students who will be drafting their own picture books.

I look in the public library for appropriate picture books that will grab the interest of fifth grade students and lend themselves to a variety of mini-lessons for this genre study. The ethnic diversity of this class guides my selection. I check out *Grandfather's Journey* (Say 1993), *The Great Migration* (Lawrence 1993), *Tar Beach* (Ringgold 1991), *Knots on a Counting Rope* (Martin 1987), *The Wagon* (Johnston 1996), and *Camel Caravan* (Roberts 1996).

The weeks fly by. Excitement is building in the class as children draft, revise, share, and critique their pieces. Yuan has written a picture book about his first day in America and plans to enter it in a contest. The art teacher is working with him on his delicate colored pencil illustrations. (We later learn that he has won a city-wide prize with this piece, quite an achievement for a student who has been in this country less than two years!)

At our final conference before we say goodbye, Millie and I reflect on our work together. She says that students are "bouncing ideas off each other," and are "increasingly interested in the authoring act." She sees "highly motivated writers who enjoy what they are doing. This has been a memorable experience for these students. I've learned a lot about picture books, ideas for mini-lessons, and how to give better conferences to writers."

Reflecting on my work with Millie, I realize I recorded only part of what happened that contributed to our success. Millie spent time thinking about her growth as a teacher. She made room in her busy schedule to meet with me when I was in the building. She came to those meetings prepared with questions and observations that grew from the demonstration lesson or in the interval between visits. This made our discussions intense and meaningful.

Millie adopted a proactive stance to improve her conferring techniques. She shadowed me when I conferred with students during the writing workshop. She listened to see how I initiated the conference, how I responded to the student, and what I taught as I followed the model I learned from Lucy Calkins: research, decide, teach.

We don't always have teachers like Millie and Jeffrey's story illustrates what can happen when seeds are sewn in cold ground, like the peas that failed to germinate. My notebook contains a set of stories about working with Jeffrey in another fifth grade in a different Bronx, New York, school.

I am excited to work in Jeffrey's classroom because the talented, eager writers I worked with last year are there. In fourth grade this class served as a "fishbowl" for district staff developers learning about writers' notebooks. The kids worked hard, learned a lot, and acted appropriately when fourteen or fifteen extra adults visited their classroom during demonstration lessons. Many of them are excellent writers who know a lot about the writing process.

Now, these students are a year older and have a new teacher. The dynamics in the group are totally different. I should have known it would be that way since I realized years ago that each teacher creates his own individual classroom climate. Jeffrey's behavior confuses me, and I sense a bad omen when he says he doesn't have time to meet for planning or reflection on what happens during my visits. The students are like strangers. Have they forgotten what they learned? Last year's fluent writers seem frozen, even sullen, and their writing is wooden. Where are the sparks from fourth grade?

Time is going by, many things seem wrong. I am uncomfortable about Jeffrey's relationships with students. No writing is generated between visits. Notebooks look the same as they did when I left the previous week.

When I am teaching the mini-lesson Jeffrey may talk to students or leave the room. He doesn't seem to understand that I am there to teach him. I try to corner him in the teachers' room before school in the morning, but we need a private place to talk.

It is my second year in the school, so I know several teachers who would welcome me in their classrooms. I make an appointment with the principal. As I meet with her, I try not to put Jeffrey in a compromised position. I say that he may have misunderstood how much time it would take to work with me and seems busy with mandated things. I suggest that I use a second first grade class as a demonstration site so that the two first grade teachers can work, share, and reinforce each other as they learn from me. However, my ideas fall on deaf ears, and I continue in Jeffrey's class.

During my eighth visit, Monaye whispers that Jeffrey is writing and illustrating a picture book that he is planning to send to a publisher. What a piece of news. At the end of class, I inquire about his book. He turns coy, but is willing to talk about it. When I ask if he has shared his book with the class, he looks puzzled. I inquire if he would be willing to read his book and receive comments from the students next week? Though seemingly reluctant, he agrees to do so.

Today is my next to last visit. Jeffrey, blushing and nervously clearing his throat, reads his book and shows his illustrations. The students are mesmerized—their teacher is an author. They reveal their knowledge about authoring as they offer insightful comments and suggestions. If only I could get Jeffrey to build on this experience. We talk after class for those few minutes we can snatch, but it seems evident that he will be unable, at least for now, to see the connection between his own writing and his teaching of writing.

These stories represent the extremes and there are many mentoring experiences that fall in the middle between Jeffrey and Millie, but these extreme examples illustrate the importance of the choice of protégé for staff development work. Jeffrey's story is all the more disheartening because the very same group of young writers had blossomed so beautifully the previous year.

COLLEGIALITY: THE COMPANION PLANTING

Rethinking Jeffrey's story, many elements were missing or simply wrong. I failed to become a colleague who could help him with his learning. He kept me at a distance, so we did not develop that collegial relationship. Our small discussions were snatched at the beginning or end of a demonstration lesson when students were present. Jeffrey wasn't aware of how powerful it would be to use his own writing experiences in his teaching.

A mentoring relationship is like a fragile bud that needs to be protected against possible cold spring weather. Classroom teachers need that same protection and nurturing because they have so many demands on their time and energy. A mentor needs to recognize and validate where a protégé is in her thinking, what she is ready to learn. My job is to open doors, make suggestions, be a role model. Where I begin, how I establish the collegial relationship is essential to how the work will develop. I sometimes suspend my agenda to listen to the real concerns of a protégé that may or may not fit directly into the work.

In my role as a retired teacher mentor in Westport, I first met Kate Sanderson, a beginning first grade teacher, when I picked her up at the train station one August day. She had not yet moved from the city and had no car. Here are notes I made:

> We park at Coleytown School and walk into the classroom. What a shock. I think she might cry. The room is stripped bare: no furniture, no books, no materials. The first thing we do is look on the stage where unused furniture is stored and ask the custodian for moving assistance. We find bright paper to cover the dull, brown bulletin boards and make an appointment with the principal to talk about ordering materials. Ann Sklar, another first grade teacher, generously offers to share things she has ordered and already re-

ceived. I leave Kate to work in her room and go to the public library where I check out a large collection of books for her classroom. At the end of a long day, Kate remarks that we are trying to turn a house into a home. We plan to work tomorrow and talk about how to begin her first days with students.

While Kate and I set up her classroom, we discussed different room arrangements and started to make a list of materials she would request. We talked about observing children and getting started with activities that would help children feel comfortable. Our conversation deepened the following week as we got into more specifics. Kate and I were on our way to a communicative, warm working relationship.

FIRST STEPS: TURNING THE SOIL AND ADDING COMPOST

I must get to know the teacher and the classroom in specific, concrete ways if I am to be helpful. This important needs assessment helps me focus on the strengths of the protégé as our work begins. In the initial conversation I try to learn some of the following things about the protégé:

- What does she value in teaching?
- Why is she working with me? Did she volunteer or was she "volunteered"?
- How much does she know about children's literature?
- Is she familiar with professional literature?
- What is her teaching background?
- What structures has she put in place for classroom management?
- What is her stance as a learner? Is she comfortable with new ideas? What is she ready to try?

Starting in a New Classroom: Planting Seeds and Seedlings

My work for The Reading and Writing Project is not usually with beginning staff. Before I visit a new Writing Project site, I try to set up a schedule with the administrator that includes demonstration lessons plus time to discuss those lessons and plan with protégés. During my first visit, I ask for a class list because I want to become familiar with names to help me model the importance of observing children. I use my notebook to record observations and make certain the protégé sees how my notebook helps me learn and teach.

The classroom needs a well-established meeting area. At my first demonstration lesson, if necessary, I teach how to gather together and listen to each other. I talk with the protégé about the importance of a strong classroom community. I establish rules for listening and sharing. I may begin a reference chart, "How To Be a Good Listener." Establishing guidelines with students helps to model three things: how to set up a new structure for the classroom, what is reasonable to expect from students, and how to begin a reference chart. (For additional discussion of reference charts, see Chapter 3.)

I demonstrate the use of a quiet voice with positive comments. If I hear or see unacceptable behavior on the part of students or my protégé, I add these items to our agenda for discussion. These are sensitive issues that need to be carefully addressed. Leslie, for example, was an excellent second grade teacher and learner. But her voice was strident and it was obvious to me that some of her young students were intimidated when she raised her voice to get their attention. I taught the class attention-getting signals, counting to three quietly, and hands up for quiet, flicking the lights once, clapping. I demonstrated to Leslie that an effective way to decrease the noise level was to lower my voice and talk under the children.

I carefully explain my reasons for making any new move. For example, if I do a whip, which is going quickly around the circle to listen to everyone's writing topics at the end of the workshop, I do not assume that a teacher will automatically understand why I did it. I explain that this is a way to help students think of topics. If the whip is designed to listen to evaluative comments about independent reading books, I explain how this helps the other readers in the classroom. I use my notebook to help me remember what we need to discuss and, as I note specific examples, what I need to plan.

TRUST AND CONFIDENTIALITY: SUNSHINE AND WATER

Trust is essential to a collegial relationship as sunshine and water are to the growth of a garden. Trust is essential because as it increases so does risk-taking on the part of the protégé. If the purpose of the relationship between the mentor and the protégé is growth, then it is important that the protégé be willing to step to the end of the diving board and take the plunge. For example, I need to be trusted with students. When I had my own classroom, if I didn't trust a visitor, I was resentful of the intrusion. I assume that protégés feel the same way. Trust will grow as I make accurate observations of students and share them with the teacher. It can grow as I respond to the protégé's interests and needs. It will get stronger as the protégé sees the excitement students feel about reading and/or writing workshop.

I try not to violate any of the structures that a protégé has put in place. I let him show me how he gets the attention of students, how he achieves transitions from one activity to another, and how he handles disciplinary problems before I offer any suggestions. If I plan to add to his repertoire in these areas, it is important to have convincing reasons about why things might be done differently.

A protégé needs to trust that I will demonstrate new ideas that are reasonable and practical so the introduction of anything new is carefully structured. In my work with The Writing Project, for example, if I am teaching the use of writers' notebooks, I begin in a way that will help teacher and students feel this is something they can do. I may read a story or two from *Henry and Mudge* (Rylant 1987) and talk about how Cynthia Rylant finds her writing ideas in everyday life. I may say, "Just as Cynthia Rylant does, I know you all have stories to tell. Do you have a cat? Do you feed it, play with it? What does it look like? What's its name?" Or, "Do you have a baby brother or sister at home? Does the baby wake you up at night?" "Do you have an older sister or brother who tells you what to do?" As the children join the conversation we begin to make a reference chart. The title may be "What I Can Write About in My Notebook." The class will add to this chart as new ideas surface. In the classroom where students choose their own topics, ideas for writing topics come as quickly as bubbles rising to the top of a glass of seltzer.

A teacher must know that I will not break confidences that are shared as we work together because confidential information about students, peers, or administrators will come up. As we begin the mentor/protégé relationship, I discuss the importance of trust and how I plan to honor it as our work develops. Trust is an underpinning to our eventual success.

SUPPORT: STAKING THE PLANTS

Just as I stake plants in my garden so they can grow strong and not topple over as they reach toward the sun, I try to convey from the start that I am there to lend a hand, to help, to support in whatever way I can. Support does not mean that constructive criticism is absent, but if a protégé knows that support underlies our work, she will be better able to accept that criticism as I nudge her toward more effective teaching.

Mentor Support

Support for a beginning teacher may be in the form of finding furniture and books for an empty classroom, rehearsing a conference with an administrator, listening to the protégé talk about something that troubles her, or helping with information about a child prior to a parent conference. From my journal:

> Susan is understandably nervous about meeting with Margaret's mother. Mrs. T. has a reputation in the school as a troublesome parent. During a meeting, Susan expresses concern about what she will say to Mrs. T. about Margaret's reading. I offer to do a reading evaluation of Margaret.
>
> Margaret and I have a good time as I interview her about reading. She knows a lot about choosing books and about reading strategies. She says the way to figure out new words is to "sound them out." She loves to read but feels nervous about reading aloud for fear of making a mistake. After the warm-up interview, Margaret chooses a book to read with me. I ask her to pick one that is a comfortable read. We talk about strategies she can use when she comes to a word she doesn't know.
>
> I photocopy my observation notes for Susan. In the interview Margaret was very focused on "sounding out" which is not the only strategy that works for young readers. I suggest that Margaret may feel uncomfortable about reading aloud at home and that it might help Margaret if Susan shared with Mrs. T. other strategies for reading unknown words. She could also discuss the idea of not putting pressure on Margaret but helping her to build confidence and pleasure in reading by doing more silent reading.

This story is meant to demonstrate that support can come in many forms besides the traditional demonstration lesson. Time is well-invested in helping a teacher unlock a bothersome problem. The purpose of working with Margaret was to help Susan prepare a conference and learn more about how to diagnose a child's reading. My notes will help her remember what she can do.

There are other ways to support protégés. For example, I like one way used by my friend, Caltha Crowe, who is doing staff development now in Westport. She sends the teacher a note after a meeting or visit. The note reviews important points covered in the demonstration lesson and/or the discussion. The note is intended to help protégés review and clarify what occurred during Caltha's visit.

Administrative Support

When a mentor begins work in a building, it is important to have administrative support. Part of that support is the choice of teachers with whom to work. Jeffrey's story illustrates a lack of administrative support. He should not have been chosen or, at the least, a different teacher could have been substituted when it became obvious that Jeffrey would not benefit from the staff development work.

Leah Rukeyser, principal of the Columbus Magnet School in New Rochelle, New York, supports my work by listening to my suggestions and modifying them to fit her objectives. For example, the third year I worked in that school I suggested that I might work again with protégés I taught earlier. I had thought of several visits to each classroom. Leah modified this idea by scheduling one hour during each of my days at Columbus to discuss problems or make plans with a former protégé. This gave former protégés new support as they continued to develop their teaching skills.

Teachers need administrative support when they are taking risks and trying new things. They want their administrators to understand that they are making the effort to become even better teachers. An administrator can help teachers in the following ways:

- providing supportive listening when teachers need to talk over their problems and/or their new learning
- arranging schedules so that peer groups can meet
- purchasing books and materials for the classroom
- purchasing professional books
- attending peer group meetings to lend support
- encouraging teachers to seek inservice credit for study group work
- approving attendance at professional conferences

I encourage protégés to discuss successes as well as problems with administrators. A good professional book or article can be shared with an administrator. If a peer group had an interesting discussion, the principal could hear about it in a brief note or a casual conversation in the hall. If a group of students responded positively to a new strategy a teacher tried, it is a good idea to mention it when the opportunity arises. A tuned-in administrator will provide better support for protégés who demonstrate enthusiasm and growth.

Peer Support

When planting a garden, it's important, for example, to put all the bean seeds together in one place so they can be staked easily. A peer group provides the fencing for protégés to lean on as they share ideas, strategies, books, minilessons, and student work that results from successful classroom experiences.

Establishing a peer group takes work and time. I have experimented with making it a precondition for my work with protégés, but I think the optimum conditions for a peer group are reached when attendance is voluntary, as it is at Columbus Magnet School. Offering inservice credit is an incentive for attending peer group meetings.

Meetings held on the same day and at the same time are best. It helps when one teacher takes the role of facilitator and schedules meeting times, photocopies articles to be discussed, arranges for different members to bring food. When teachers are excited about learning, they will find time—at lunch, before or after school. Setting up a peer group is a good early move for a staff developer because a strong group will help guarantee that the work of examining and trying new practices will continue after the mentor has left the building.

GOALS: THE HARVEST

In a paper, "Connecticut's Professional Educator Development Program" (Connecticut Department of Education 1990), the underlying beliefs of the program are stated as follows:

> An excellent experienced teacher engages in *reflection,* possesses a *repertoire* of skills, and accepts professional *responsibilities* beyond the classroom.
>
> Becoming a reflective practitioner, while at the same time expanding one's repertoire, is a developmental process that begins during one's teacher preparation and continues throughout one's professional career.

THE GOAL OF A MENTORING RELATIONSHIP IS TO HELP A protégé expand his teaching repertoire and have it snowball in the classroom where it has an effect on children. It may be a repertoire for classroom management, using writers' notebooks, teaching reading strategies, working with parents, or a combination of these. Whatever the specific goal, the purpose is to help the protégé learn procedures that will become a part of her teaching life.

The bergamot in my garden flourishes when it is carefully tended throughout the growing season and covered with leaves to keep it from freezing in the winter. Protégés need nurturing throughout their professional lives so they remain enthusiastic about learning. If they have successful experiences that prove valuable in their daily work, they are more likely to seek out learning opportunities throughout their teaching careers and their lives.

CONDITIONS FOR BEGINNING
A SUCCESSFUL MENTORING EXPERIENCE

- choice of protégés
- establishment of collegiality
- learning about the protégé (needs assessment)
- establishing trust and confidentiality
- support from:

  mentor

  administration

  peers

REFERENCES

Connecticut Department of Education. 1990. "Connecticut's Professional Educator Development Program, A Prospectus." Hartford, CT.

Johnston, Tony. 1996. *The Wagon.* New York: Tambourine.

Lawrence, Jacob. 1993. *The Great Migration: An American Story.* New York, Museum of Modern Art and Washington, D.C., Phillips Collection. New York: Harper Collins.

Martin, Bill. 1987. *Knots on a Counting Rope.* New York: Henry Holt.

Ringgold, Faith. 1991. *Tar Beach.* New York: Crown.

Roberts, Bethany. 1996. *Camel Caravan.* New York: Tambourine.

Rylant, Cynthia. 1987. *Henry and Mudge.* New York: Bradbury Press.

Say, Allen. 1993. *Grandfather's Journey.* Boston: Houghton Mifflin.

Shanker, Albert. 1995. *The New York Times.* "Sink or Swim." February 22.

2

Nurturing Professional Growth

A skillful gardener toils to overcome conditions outside his control, such as lack of rain or deer with voracious appetites. The mentoring relationship may also contain ingredients that cannot be controlled by either the mentor or the protégé, or both. But, there are some things we can try to achieve as best we can. This chapter considers conditions and strategies that can nurture the mentoring relationship and help a protégé along the road to growth and change.

QUALITY TIME

In my garden, I am not always interested in flashy annuals that blossom early and die. My goal is to carefully tend to perennials that return year after year becoming ever richer and more abundant. Growing a garden takes time as does the quality learning that comes from a carefully tended mentoring relationship.

A relationship between mentor and protégé needs time for roots to grow, deepen, and become strong. When I have had the opportunity to return to a school a second or third year for The Reading and Writing Project, I began to see this kind of growth. I talk with the administrator about working again with the same protégés. This is not easy for principals to support because, unlike the experienced gardener who works the soil, composting regularly to create the richest growing environment possible, principals are tempted to ask the mentor to work with new teachers rather than deepening the relationship with former protégés. I try to sell the idea that protégés need the time to explore, test, revise, and revisit new ideas. Working with them a

16

second year can result in lasting learning that makes more of a difference in the lives of students.

The mentor's daily schedule in a school may be out of her control. I lobby to get enough time for demonstration lessons followed by discussion time with the protégé. This means a mentor usually cannot teach in more than four classrooms in one day. Administrators get more mileage from a mentor's visits when they arrange for coverage so additional teachers can observe in demonstration sites and participate in discussions.

Classroom visits should be a minimum of forty-five minutes so that the lesson can include enough time for reading or writing on the part of students. The mentor acts as a role model for the protégé as he works with students. He models skills in classroom management, teaching mini-lessons, observing and conferring with individual students, and conducting share time.

As teachers aspire to be more effective, mentor and protégé need time to discuss:

- individual students
- plans for demonstration lessons
- what the protégé will do between visits
- other issues that arise as they work together

Here's a conversation from my notebook that could not be rushed but needed the time to develop:

> Jim asks me how I decide with whom to confer. I begin by sharing my record-keeping strategies to make sure I don't consistently miss anyone. Also, I share how I observe children, or do kidwatching, to determine who needs immediate help. I encourage Jim to try these ideas. We talk about putting a sign up on the chalkboard during the workshop period with three spaces, so students can request a conference and continue their work while they wait.

PACING

Staff development needs to be paced so the work will ripen completely. This can't be achieved if the work is too rushed or if I wait too long. For example, when the staff development work is paced too quickly there is a lot of pressure on the protégé who may still need additional support when the mentoring must come to an end. My Reading and Writing Project work is usually a minimum of ten visits, which is satisfactory when the visits are stretched over at least ten weeks. The Westport work is done during a whole school year, which is even better.

Mentor visits should not be scheduled too closely together. Protégés need the opportunity to think about and practice new ideas between visits and to imagine and develop questions they want to discuss with the mentor. At the same time, the protégé needs to be clear about what her responsibilities are between visits.

I had a total of fifteen days to work as a mentor at a school in the Bronx. I arranged the work in two parts. The first part consisted of ten Tuesdays in November, December, and January. The second part consisted of five days in late March and April. This allowed the protégés two months to work without me. Three of the four protégés worked hard and pushed their thinking in new directions during the interval. In March, they were ready to learn even more based upon the solid ground of two months of practice.

AVAILABILITY

A mentor cannot always be available for the protégé, but sometimes it is important to clear the schedule to help out. Beth, a beginning teacher, was confronted with a sudden and tragic death when Jeremy, one of her young students, lost his mother. Beth made mature judgments about how to handle the situation but needed a listener to confirm her thinking and add new ideas.

Beth and I took a long walk after school to talk about Jeremy and the other children. Things were going as well as could be expected, except when a child said something to Jeremy that Beth considered cruel or unnecessary. The most difficult part was the parents. Several of them had come to Beth wanting to talk because they needed to share their anxieties.

Beth felt her job was to be Jeremy's advocate, to shield him from careless conversation from either peers or parents. We decided that the best way to protect him was to refer parents to the school psychologist or the principal. It was important that I was available to listen and brainstorm when Beth needed help about problems surrounding a death that had such impact on everyone.

GIVING PROTÉGÉS RESPONSIBILITY FOR PRACTICE

I watched my granddaughter, Emily, learn to swim. She tried countless times to swim a short distance to her father. In one afternoon we could see her improve because she was so persistent about practice. As the relationship between myself and a protégé begins to grow, I ask him to take responsibility for practicing new strategies between visits. Millie and Jeffrey, discussed in Chapter 1, illustrate two extremes of teachers in relation to responsibility. Most protégés willingly take charge after the mentor has done enough coaching to help them try out new strategies.

I launched a reading response group in Nan's class. Nan knew I could not be there every day, so she asked for help with mini-lessons. The following is from my notebook:

> Nan is excited when I return this week because she has tried two ideas I suggested and one of her own. Close observation of students helped her realize that the class needed to talk about how to include everyone in response group discussions. She did role-playing mini-lessons in which she and a student played the parts of children in a response group. First, she played the role of a quiet student and asked the class to suggest how the group leader could encourage her to participate. Then she acted as an aggressive student as the class made suggestions about how to help her with self-control. Nan is pleased because she met the problem head on.

FEEDBACK

In the beginning, protégés will be more comfortable teaching lessons without having an observer. But it is important to discuss what's happening. What did she teach? What did she observe? What kind of follow-up has she planned? After a comfort level is reached, the mentor can observe the protégé and give feedback. If possible, I like to let the protégé decide when she is ready to invite me in.

Dr. Henry Drewry, Director of the Teacher Preparation Program at Princeton University, in a paper entitled "Mentoring and The Professional Development of Beginning Teachers," said, "Success in providing feedback will depend in large part on the overall relationship between mentor and beginning teacher. . . . Specific techniques will differ but a guiding principle must be the establishment of mutual trust, integrity, and professional rapport." Specific feedback about classroom management, mini-lessons, how the protégé works with students, and record keeping helps protégés refine their practices. This feedback should be grounded in realistic goals for protégé growth.

RECORD KEEPING

I give protégés responsibility for keeping notebooks and provide mine as a model. I write in it continuously to record:

- mini-lessons taught
- student writing topics and book choices

- notes about individual students
- names of students with whom I conferred
- ideas for future demonstration lessons as a result of kidwatching
- agenda items for meetings
- notes about what transpires during meetings
- reminders to bring an article, to find a book, or to do something for a future visit

An easy way for a protégé to begin keeping a journal is by doing a focused observation of a child. This is from my notebook:

> Lisa says she has never been good at record keeping. I suggest that recording in her notebook may help us find ways to help Luis. Lisa agrees to try but asks how I manage to write down so much. I tell her about my own shorthand techniques: *r* for reading, *w* for writing, omitting vowels, such as *wnt* for *went* and *pln* for *plan*.
>
> Lisa's recording shows that Luis spends a lot of writing time talking to Carlos who is annoyed because he can't work. Lisa decides Luis needs to become more independent and take responsibility for his writing.

As soon as Lisa got accustomed to writing in her notebook, she began to keep a record of the books she read aloud because she thought that would help her planning. She started to make notes during the writers' share to discover who was contributing and who was not. We used her notebook as a focal point for our discussions as we began to fine tune her practice.

Some protégés have tried double entry notebooks to help with planning. Figure 2.1 is an example of a double entry notebook.

EXPLICIT TEACHING

When I drive on the interstate, I expect other drivers to use their directional signals to tell me their intentions. If they don't, it is confusing and an accident could occur. As I drive the staff development road, I try to signal my intentions and be explicit about why I do things and what my plans and expectations are when I work in a protégé's classroom.

For example, I use agreed upon signs rather than a loud voice to get quiet in the room because I want the tone and mood to be one of self-control. I create a meeting area because I think students listen better to each other when they are close and feel the power of the group. I don't repeat what a child says because I want students to listen to each other, not to me alone. I try not to take anything for granted. I talk about each strategy so the

Lesson	Observation Notes
12/4/96 Mini-lesson: "hot words" (adjectives)	
1. Write three nouns students use in writing on chart: *dog, birthday, brother.*	Children excited because they can read words.
2. Talk about hot words to give reader better picture. Give examples: *brown dog, small brown dog, wet hungry dog.*	Children attentive. Seem to understand concept. Begin to make suggestions.
3. Have children add hot words to *birthday* and *brother.* Use chart.	Good suggestions: *exciting sixth birthday, tall older brother.*
4. Invite children to use two hot words in their writing today. Suggest they underline them so they can find them easily.	Ben, Emily, and Michael anxious to begin writing.
5. Share will focus on hot words students use today. 6. Share.	Ben, Emily, Jana, Adam, and Michael share examples. Paul, Andrea, Tim, and Kerry don't have a clue. Help them tomorrow.
12/5/96 Demonstrate how authors use hot words. Read *Spinky Sulks,* Steig (1988) during morning meeting. Point out and discuss specific examples from book.	Children love book. They remember: *slimy voice, no fake kiss, stupid family.*
Writing workshop: mini-lesson	Examples supplied by kids: *fat mean sister, helpful kind friend, yelling ugly mean sister.*
1. Add more examples on chart using nouns: *sister, friend, cat.* 2. Invite children to continue using hot words in their writing. Suggest they underline them.	Helped Andrea, Paul, and Tim. Maybe Andrea and Tim understand.
3. Explain that share will focus on hot words used today. 4. Share examples at end of writing workshop.	Andrea and Tim share. Will, Andrew, Jamie, and Jesse share. Ben shows off writing string of six adjectives with the noun *brother.* Continue tomorrow.

Figure 2.1 An example of a double entry notebook

protégé will understand it and practice it in his own way. Here's a story from my notebook:

> Jake is struggling with control of his fourth grade students. He seems more like a puppeteer trying to pull strings rather than a lead player in the classroom show. I share my observations with Jake and we agree to work together to get a tighter reign on the class.
>
> Jake and I establish signals to use when a few students are out of control or when the whole class needs a reminder. Jake agrees he needs to consistently follow through with these signals. We discuss his demeanor. I feel he would create respect if he lowered his voice and was consistent in his expectations. I suggest that he explicitly model respectful conversation while he points to what he is doing. Jake is planning to work on the classroom community by introducing special activities such as a morning meeting in which everyone participates as an equal, including Jake.

THE ROLE OF REFLECTION

Reflection is central to the work between mentor and protégé. Without reflection, it would be as if I planted the seeds in my garden but blocked out the sun and neglected to water them. "Real learning only occurs when teachers participate in a reflective analysis of their lessons. Mentors must then help teachers adapt new knowledge to what they already know" (*The Mentor Teacher Casebook,* p. 29). I cannot assume a protégé includes reflection in her day—in fact, it is easy to overlook it because of the pressure cooker pace of school life. I comment on this in my notebook:

> I encourage Sandra to reflect on the behavior of children. We discuss Carl who seems unable to write down beginning sounds. I ask if he cannot do this or if he craves attention so much that he waits for a teacher to work with him. Sandra assumes he can't do it. I suggest she get him started tomorrow, stay with him a few minutes and ask him to work independently. She can tell him that she will return later to see how he is getting along. She needs to try this strategy a few days to test whether this will help him become more independent.

Here's another example from the same class:

> Sandra and I observe that Sylvia and Robert have a hard time coming to the meeting area. We brainstorm ways to help Sylvia first. Sandra says she thinks Sylvia likes children to focus on her. She will try holding her hand when it is time to gather. Sandra remarks that Julio is always bothering people when he sits down in the meeting area. I suggest she talk to him be-

fore they move and say that she expects him to sit near her quietly and be ready to listen. We come to the conclusion that working with those two children is enough for now, so Sandra will postpone focusing on Robert.

If a protégé is not naturally reflective, then my goal is to help him learn to be so. Reflection is necessary if we are to teach protégés how to ground their teaching in the individual needs of students. Reflection is thinking back, in order to think ahead. It is central to short- and long-term planning.

FLEXIBILITY

I learned to be flexible in my own classroom when what happened there began to inform my daily teaching. The learning demonstrated by children each day, plus the emotional and social needs that came to the foreground, could radically alter my plans. Flexibility is an important stance for a mentor to model as protégés reveal their strengths and weaknesses. Here's a story from my notebook:

> Last week I asked the study group members to read an article from *Language Arts* so we could discuss it today, but as the meeting begins, many said they didn't bring the article. We agree to postpone the discussion a week until our next meeting. I turn the conversation to the next item on our agenda. We have a spirited and helpful discussion about titles to use as touchstone books with everyone contributing because I use the "turn to the person next to you" strategy and then ask each person to share what her partner said. Before we leave I point out that I have modeled the kind of flexibility we need to show in classrooms.

PROFESSIONAL READING AND CONFERENCES

My professional reading and attendance at conferences is a model for protégés when I share articles, books, or conference notes. I file copies of articles and notes by topics: spelling, first grade, the classroom community. If an article fits under two topics, I duplicate it twice and file it in both places to help me locate it easily.

My favorite professional books have chapters that lend themselves to discussion and thinking about classroom problems. I use the following books often:

- *A Fresh Look at Writing* (Graves 1994)
- *. . . And with a Light Touch* (Avery 1993)

- *A Teacher's Sketch Journal, Observations on Learning and Teaching* (Ernst 1997)
- *The Art of Teaching Writing* (Calkins 1994)
- *Creating Classrooms for Authors and Inquirers* (Short, Harste, and Burke 1995)
- *On Their Way, Celebrating Second Graders as They Read and Write* (Fraser and Skolnick 1994)
- *Spelling in Use* (Laminack and Wood 1996)
- *Teaching Children to Care, Management in the Responsive Classroom* (Charney 1992)
- *Thinking and Learning Together* (Fisher 1995)

I may lend my copy of a book to a protégé or duplicate pages from it. If she likes it, I recommend that she purchase the book or ask her administrator to get it for the school's professional library.

When I attend the fall National Council of Teachers of English meeting, I browse through the book exhibit to see what new books will help in my work. In addition, I transcribe my notes from speakers at the conference so that I can share these notes with protégés. This creates the opportunity to talk about taking the time to attend professional conferences.

CHILDREN'S LITERATURE

Children's books are a springboard for my staff development work, so I cruise the book exhibit at professional conferences looking at new titles and some-times talking with authors. My local public library is another place where I keep up with what's new. The librarians have a special shelf for new books, so I look there when I go into the children's department.

I like to share my knowledge of children's literature with protégés. Millie, the teacher I spoke about in Chapter 1, was not too familiar with picture books and appreciated the introduction I gave her. We talked about how she could expand her knowledge of picture books. Laura, a second grade teacher in the Bronx, became so interested in children's books that each week I visited her classroom I saw new books she had purchased. Her principal was helping her with some of the expense, but Laura was hooked and spent a lot of her own money.

THE MENTOR AS MODEL

I try to be a reading and writing role model for protégés and students. Using my own writing for mini-lessons is not an original idea, but it is a very effective teaching tool. I am a better writing teacher because I write. Experience has taught me what hard work it is. I think about where I get ideas, how I construct a piece, and how I go about the steps of revision. I think about my reading: how books influence my writing, how I choose books, what I do when I'm not interested in a book, what I do when I come to an unknown word, when I skim, and when I read closely.

As a role model, I discuss with protégés how I:

- examine my reading and writing
- choose mini-lessons
- work with students during reading or writing workshop
- monitor my tone of voice
- write in my journal
- observe and relate to students

"By being shown how to teach a lesson, a teacher gains access to a new model of instruction. It is always important to discuss and analyze the lesson after the modeling has occurred, and to help the teacher to adapt the technique to her own pedagogical practice" (*The Mentor Teacher Casebook,* p. 39).

PEERS AS MODELS

A peer can be a model for a beginning or a more experienced teacher. At PS 96 in the Bronx, Lisa Duffy and her next-door neighbor discussed writing workshop, shared their discoveries about children's books, and visited in each other's rooms to learn from each other. Beginning teacher protégés learn by visiting the classrooms of more experienced colleagues. The administrator can facilitate these visits by arranging coverage for a teacher to facilitate visiting within the school or across town. The dialogue that develops between teachers lessens the sense of isolation people feel in the classroom. Over the years, I have noticed a pattern of problems that develop around workshop teaching, the behavior problems students present, and classroom organization issues. Seasoned practitioners, as well as beginning teachers, benefit from discussing these issues with peers (see Chapter 8, peer coaching).

IN THIS CHAPTER, I DISCUSSED CONDITIONS AND STRATEGIES that nurture protégé growth after the relationship has begun. The following chart summarizes what helps a professional mentor/protégé relationship grow into a meaningful partnership. The mentor's job is to help protégés learn new repertoires they can use over time to benefit the children in their classrooms.

OPTIMAL CONDITIONS	TEACHING STRATEGIES
• quality time	• giving responsibility to protégé
• appropriate pacing	• providing feedback
• availability of mentor	• demonstrating record keeping
	• being explicit about teaching strategies
	• encouraging reflection
	• demonstrating flexibility
	• sharing professional reading and conferences
	• sharing children's literature
	• being a role model
	• encouraging peer role models

REFERENCES

Avery, Carol. 1993. . . . *And with a Light Touch, Learning About Reading, Writing and Teaching with First Graders.* Portsmouth, NH: Heinemann.

Calkins, Lucy. 1994. *The Art of Teaching Writing.* Portsmouth, NH: Heinemann.

Charney, Ruth Sidney. 1992. *Teaching Children to Care, Management in the Responsive Classroom.* Greenfield, MA: Northeast Foundation for Children.

Drewry, Henry. 1988. "Mentoring and The Professional Development of Beginning Teachers." Unpublished paper.

Ernst, Karen. 1997. *A Teacher's Sketch Journal, Observations on Learning and Teaching.* Portsmouth, NH: Heinemann.

Fisher, Bobbi. 1995. *Thinking and Learning Together.* Portsmouth, NH: Heinemann.

Fraser, Jane and Donna Skolnick. 1994. *On Their Way, Celebrating Second Graders as They Read and Write.* Portsmouth, NH: Heinemann.

Graves, Donald H. 1994. *A Fresh Look at Writing.* Portsmouth, NH: Heinemann.

Laminack, Lester L. and Katie Wood. 1996. *Spelling in Use.* Urbana, IL: National Council of Teachers of English.

Short, Kathy G., Jerome C. Harste, with Carolyn Burke. 1995. *Creating Classrooms for Authors and Inquirers.* Portsmouth, NH: Heinemann.

Shulman, Judith H. and Joel A. Colbert, eds. 1987. *The Mentor Teacher Casebook.* San Francisco, CA: Far West Laboratory for Educational Research and Development. Eugene, OR: ERIC Clearinghouse on Educational Management.

Steig, William. 1988. *Spinky Sulks.* New York: Farrar, Straus and Giroux.

3

Creating a Classroom That Works

*F*riends were coming for dinner so I decided to bake a scrumptious cake I had not made in years. As I put the mixed ingredients in the pan, the texture felt wrong, it was too runny. But I talked myself into believing that the texture was the same as it used to be, that I just didn't remember accurately. I put the cake in the oven and turned around to see the flour sitting on the counter, unused. The most basic ingredient was missing. Sometimes a classroom can feel like a cake without flour. The texture is not right. It may be too fluid, not glued together.

A TEACHER MAKES HUNDREDS OF DECISIONS EVERY DAY— about students, curriculum, pacing, his choice of words and deeds. These decisions help create a positive, well-functioning classroom community when the flour is there, when things stick together and rise gently as they are cooked. Mentors frequently need to help fold flour into the mix. This chapter is a discussion of classroom organization and management ideas I have modeled and discussed in detail with protégés in attempts to achieve just the right classroom texture.

CONSISTENCY

Children thrive in a supportive, predictable environment. In a consistent classroom students feel confident because they can rely on dependable structures. They know their teacher will treat everyone fairly and with empathy.

This kind of learning environment encourages both achievement and risk taking while it provides for individual differences.

Starting the Day

In a consistent classroom, each day begins in a predictable way. The teacher recognizes that it is important to renew the feeling of safety and help students regain their comfort each morning. This includes letting them know what will be expected of them that day.

A morning message can help everyone settle in and get engaged in a meaningful activity. Here is an example, from a second grade classroom the morning after a cultural arts assembly:

March 19, 1997

Dear Class,

You were an excellent audience at yesterday's program. Please write a letter home. Explain what you liked best about the program and why you liked that part.

Enjoy your day at school.

At Coleytown School in Westport, Sarah Merriman helps Tracie DeLawrence think through how to begin her morning by suggesting activities adapted from *The Responsive Classroom* (Charney, Clayton, and Wood 1995). Sarah describes how her students stand in a circle and greet each other with a chant, a song, or a ritualized game with a ball. As everyone learns the pattern, a challenge can be introduced in how the circle is arranged. For example, one day students stand alphabetically by first name, another by last name. Sarah has instructions written on the chalkboard when students arrive in the room.

When I taught second grade, my favorite activity after the morning meeting was to read aloud to the class. The shared experience of a good read aloud reunited our community before we launched into our busy day. The morning message, meeting, and read aloud can all be included in any ritual or pattern of activities that takes the first fifteen minutes of the school day.

Class Rules

It is appropriate for protégés to begin the discussion of class rules on the first day of school. When rules are agreed upon, they can be written on a reference chart and hung up in the classroom. Each member of the class can sign the chart to complete the contract. (See the section in this chapter on reference charts.)

I helped Debbie, a fourth grade teacher in the Bronx, as students constructed a web, "Values for Our Class," which we photocopied for each child to keep at her desk. The ideas reflected the values of students, school, teacher, and parent community. The web included:

- Always try to do your best work.
- Don't say "I can't do it."
- Be organized.
- Don't give up.
- Ask if there's something that you don't understand.
- Be serious about your work.

Other Issues to Consider

Consistency is subtly enhanced by the details of classroom organization. When helping a protégé achieve a consistent structure in his classroom, consider setting up:

- clearly defined tasks for work
- routines for discussions (see section in this chapter)
- signals for getting attention
- expectations for use of materials
- distribution and putting away of materials
- expectations for arrival and dismissal
- transitions, such as moving from desks to meeting area, getting ready for gym
- behavioral expectations around the school
- procedures for going to bathroom, going to the library, signing up for writers' share, etc.
- the room arranged to enhance workshop learning (see section in this chapter)
- routines for attendance, lunch orders, etc.
- rules for playground equipment

MOTIVATING STUDENTS

Years ago, a consultant who worked in our district described teaching as a "science-based performing art." My interpretation of these words is that the science base is what you can learn in courses and the performing art is the intuitive part based on personality, sense of timing, voice, understanding of students' needs, and personal relationships.

Sparkle and Challenge

Peter's classroom had little performing art. Students were automatons who moved silently to do the minimum in response to Peter's flat affect. I wrote the following in my notebook:

> March 14: I'd like to set off some fireworks here to get the kids talking to each other. Tomorrow we'll start with random partners to discuss how they choose a writing topic. I'll role play with a student to set up guidelines. I'll ask Peter to observe and make notes for our discussion.
>
> March 21: Mini-lesson to continue partner work based on Peter's surprisingly insightful observations. Each child will turn to the person sitting beside her at her table. Partners will explain plans for writing after first jotting them down on a piece of paper. At the end of writing workshop, they will talk again about whether they followed their plans or did something different. Tomorrow Peter can build on this, doing a whip for share. The whip will consist of each student saying why he did or didn't change his plans.
>
> March 29: Peter reports that the whip idea worked well. The class had a lengthy discussion about whether they had to follow through with plans or whether it was OK to change your mind. After more trust is established, I will ask Peter if I can observe him while he teaches.
>
> April 22: Last week I coached, and today I observed Peter teach a mini-lesson on writing good endings. We need to continue our talk because his voice is still not animated enough. The lesson was too long, a problem I have, getting the mini-lesson succinct. I suggest that Peter visit Marla who challenges herself to learn new things, take risks, and try new strategies. She can be a role model.

Expectations

Communicating high expectations is a key to motivating students. Protégés and students try to live up to expectations when they know they are challenged to do their best work. This issue puzzled Lea when she began teaching. When she asked if they were doing their finest work, students always responded that they were doing the best job they could. Here are my notes:

> Lea asks about stickers. I say I am cautious about extrinsic motivations and would prefer something intrinsic. We talk about group discussions to set standards for written work. I help Lea talk with the class about writing standards and they create a reference chart. The next step is a companion chart with a rubric for effort. Then each child can use the standards plus the rubric to rate herself at the top of her paper.

Materials and Activities

A variety of materials, including books, helps motivate students. Beginning teachers may have a problem if they move into an almost empty room, as Kate Sanderson did. Borrowing from willing staff members and starting to accumulate teaching materials is something that helps protégés cheer up the room and get students interested. In Westport, we are fortunate because our public library has an excellent collection and is willing to loan large numbers of books to teachers.

I work with protégés to arrange materials and books in an enticing way that encourages students to use what is in the classroom. I help protégés demonstrate how and when to use materials during the first days in September. Books, paper, markers, scissors, and glue need to be arranged in an inviting way where they can be easily reached.

A variety of activities motivates students. Protégés need to learn how to pace their delivery of the curriculum. It needs to contain all the ingredients, such as direct teaching, time for student work and exploration, discussion, and review. It means mixing the ingredients at the proper speed, not creaming the butter and sugar at the speed needed to beat egg whites, and baking the cake at the right temperature so it will rise properly and not burn. Protégés may need help as they consider what activities are appropriate to the age and development of the students.

WORKSHOP TEACHING

Teaching readers' and writers' workshop has meant a change in the role of the teacher. The workshop teacher takes a measure of student skills as she moves through the room conferring with and teaching individuals or small groups while they work. A Board of Education member once asked me in a public meeting how many hours a day I *actually* (his emphasis) spent teaching. The implication was that when I was not covered with chalkdust I was not teaching. I explained that I was continually teaching even when students were moving in the hall, when I was speaking with parents on the phone, or at night when I was planning the next day at school. I couldn't quantify my teaching hours.

Working the Room

Workshop teachers do not stand and deliver. I model for protégés how to work the room. First, I plan and teach a mini-lesson that focuses on a specific skill or strategy. I try to keep this lesson no longer than ten minutes. It may be a response to student needs. For example, I may use *The Relatives Came* (Rylant 1985) to discuss story structure. The mini-lesson is followed by a larger block of time, perhaps thirty minutes, during which students work on their own writing. The last eight or ten minutes are given over to a writers' share when one or two children read their pieces to the group and receive a limited number of comments or questions from peers. When students are writing, the teacher is working the room, that is, she is conferring with students and teaching skills. During the share, she is recording her observations of students.

Here is a list of things a protégé can do while working the room:

READING

- Interview the student about her choice of books.
- Listen to student read for diagnostic purposes.
- Learn student's intentions or plans.
- Suggest what to read next by the same author or on the same topic.
- Help the student focus on her work.
- Pair students who can benefit from working together.
- Discuss reader response.
- Facilitate a response group.

WRITING

- Interview the student about her choice of topics.
- Learn the student's intentions or plans.
- Help the student expand, clarify, add details, improve the ending, etc.
- Review the writing conventions for which the student is responsible.
- Record the list of topics for the mini-lesson.
- Help the student focus on her work.
- Pair students who can benefit from working together.
- Facilitate editing or revision.

I WROTE THIS IN MY NOTEBOOK:

I model how I work the room for Dorothy. I invite her to shadow as I confer with students. I sit down next to James and ask, "How can I help?" Or, "I notice you are having difficulty choosing a book you like. Did you look at the list of ideas on the reference chart?" These are conversation openers. Where the conference goes depends upon James' response. I use Lucy Calkins' model in my conferring: research, decide, teach. I move in an unpredictable pattern across and around the room, conferring with as many students as possible. My record-keeping form has the names of all the children. Here is a shortened version of it:

READING CONFERENCES		
10/18-red pen	10/19-blue pen	10/21-green pen
Jesse Arin		
Emily Crystal		
Adam Michael		
Jamie Peter		
Tim Todd		

Diagnosis and Record Keeping

I try to help a protégé understand that diagnosis is an integral part of workshop teaching. It helps the teacher know:

- what mini-lessons need to be taught
- individual children who need help
- the groups of children to pull together for teaching a specific skill
- what students are thinking, learning, and planning

To learn and act on these things, a workshop teacher needs careful records. I use a combination of class lists and mailing labels. When Hildy Martin, a second grade teacher at Columbus Magnet School in New Rochelle, New York, conferred with students during writing workshop, she made notes on mailing labels (Figure 3.1).

Hildy and Janet Waller, a fourth grade teacher at the same school, put their mailing labels for one child together in a looseleaf binder so they could view them as a continuum. Figure 3.2 shows how Janet's page about Bill looked.

My notebook:

Courtney is reading *Little House in the Big Woods* (Wilder 1953). Her teacher, Kathryn, had read it aloud to the class but wonders if this book is too difficult for Courtney. I talk with Courtney as Kathryn observes. I ask why she chose the book. She responds:

Courtney: I *love* this book. It was great when Ms. S. read it to us.

Jane: What do you like about it?

Courtney: I love thinking about how people lived a long time ago.

12/4 Emma Bed to bed-retelling of events. Talked about other ways. Referred her to literature.	12/7 Mack Excellent details. Needs help with capitalizing, sentence structure.	1/11 Sophie Writing workshop now has purpose. Writes notes, letters, signs, books.
12/4 Cyndie Rich detailed writing in Spanish. Still afraid to write in English.	12/7 Nancie Won't share. Talked about it. Don't know what to do about this. Talk to Jane for suggestions?	1/11 George Winter story. Ready to edit/ publish.

Figure 3.1 Writing workshop mailing labels

Jane: Can you give me an example?

Courtney: Ugh, they played with the pig's bladder.

Jane: Will you read me some of that part?

As Courtney reads, I record on mailing labels. I note her fluency, her comprehension, words that are troublesome and ones she skips. Kathryn and I review my notes and decide how Kathryn will monitor Courtney's independent reading on a regular basis.

EXPLICIT TEACHING

An explicit teacher keeps students informed about what is going to happen and why it should happen. A teacher who is clear and explicit when talking with students creates a feeling of comfort and consistency. It is just as important for mentors to be explicit as they work with protégés as it is for protégés to give clear explanations to students. Being completely lucid helps students do better work, whether they are protégés or children.

Directions

Protégés may need help with how to give clear directions so that students understand what they are supposed to do, where to find materials, and what is expected of them. Working with students to set standards and rubrics can

10/19 Bill Editing conference. Talked about how to come up with title.	11/14 Bill's notebook. He has lots of ideas. Plays with words but writes sparsely, says a little bit re: each topic, then he's done.	12/8 Bill (with J. Fraser) re: repetition of phrase. What other ways could you say "My brother and I?" or could repeat it for emphasis—your choice as writer. Bill reads aloud and decides to leave phrases.
10/31 Bill Confer about developing piece. How to dig deeper. Show Rylant, *The Relatives Came.*	11/16 Bill How do you know when your writing is going well? "When I know what I'm going to say." Discussed this.	12/15 Bill (J. Fraser continues) Question: Do you write at home? Tell me about it. Bill says he writes stories, lists of things to do, letters to relatives.

Figure 3.2 Mailing labels for one student

help to clarify expectations. Student understanding of directions can be checked by asking a child to repeat directions: what will you do first, next, etc. I urge protégés not to choose the student who always has the record straight, but to call upon a volunteer who may need a bit of coaching.

Purpose and Intention

I urge protégés to help children understand both their purposes and intentions. By intentions I mean plans. Protégés can learn to signal their intentions throughout the school day. "We will read stories from *The House on Mango Street* (Cisneros 1984) because we will be working to make our writing more clear and concise." Or, "Let's talk about book selection strategies before we begin reading workshop so everyone has a variety of ways to choose a good book."

My notebook contains the following entry:

> Susan and I discuss how to achieve better cooperation during Status-of-the-Class. She decides to explain why she asks each student what he will be working on during Writing workshop and how this activity provides writers in the room with fresh ideas for topics. She explains that the activity gives teacher a record that she can review to help individual writers. When Susan reports a change in attitude about Status-of-the-Class, we talk about explanations of purpose for other activities. She will make a list of possible places to do this for our next discussion.

Schedule for the Day

The daily schedule should be posted and reviewed each morning. I suggest that protégés make strips of colored oak tag with the names of activities on them: science, math, computer, reading. These can be laminated and then a strip of Velcro can be put on the back of each one. The other Velcro strip is run down the wall where the schedule will be displayed. This makes it easy for a student to arrange the next day's schedule each afternoon before dismissal.

GIVING RESPONSIBILITY

Authority and control are issues for all of us. The classrooms in which we learned may have followed a metaphor I often use to describe schools of the past. Teachers were puppeteers, holding tightly onto the strings, and we were the puppets, dancing to their tunes. It is quite a challenge for us to organize our classrooms differently.

In *The New York Times Magazine* of August 17, 1997 an article by Nicholas D. Kristof on Japanese schools carried the headline, "Where Children Rule. Why are Japan's Primary Schools Better than Ours? Students Lead Classes. They even Clean Bathrooms. Everything They Learn They Teach Themselves." Japanese primary students apparently are given responsibilities we have not thought to delegate. While our schools differ, we know it is important to give students appropriate responsibilities. Notes I made:

> Cindy and I talk about cleaning up the room after using math materials. She is in despair because it is so chaotic. I make some suggestions:
>
> 1. Tell the children their help is needed and why.
> 2. Ask for their suggestions about how to improve the cleanup.

> Students decide it would be helpful to appoint a leader at each table who is responsible for making sure the materials are organized and put away. They say they will cooperate because they will want assistance when it is their turn to be responsible.

Recently I participated in a conversation between kindergarten teachers Hilda Rhodes and Mara Schwartz. They talked about how kindergarten children could help organize the class library. Books were put on the floor and the children decided what books belonged in each basket; all the bear stories in one basket, all the books about babies in another. Although this is time consuming, the activity led to familiarity with the library and better care of books.

Here is a partial list of responsibilities that protégés can help children assume:

- writing responsibilities and choices
    topic selection
    spelling and conventions appropriate to age and development
    whether to finish or abandon a piece
    when to edit, revise, publish a piece
    conferring: with whom and when
    sharing: what and when
    keeping track of materials

- reading responsibilities and choices
    book choice
    whether to finish or abandon a book
    the type and content of response
    choice of response group
    conferring: with whom and when
    sharing: what and when
    keeping track of materials

- other responsibilities and choices
    when to eat a snack
    the order in which to work on assignments
    what to do when work is complete
    when to do class job
    signing out for the bathroom, the library

The choices and responsibilities offered to students should be age appropriate. If a protégé has transferred to a new grade level or is a beginning teacher, this may be an issue as she gets acquainted with and accustomed to appropriate alternatives.

THE CLASSROOM COMMUNITY

Educators have become more sensitive to and knowledgeable about the classroom community and the impact classroom relationships have on learning. We know that shared experiences contribute to learning. If the classroom community is carefully nurtured during those first days and weeks of school, it makes a difference in the months that follow.

Here are some things that contribute to the feeling of community:

- good read alouds
- shared poetry, choral reading, chants, and songs
- classroom jokes, special sayings, or quotations
- field trips
- a spirit of fun and exploration modeled by the teacher
- choosing the Book-of-the-Week (see Chapter 7)
- validation of everyone's ideas to create a feeling of safety, "I like when Evan said . . . It helped me realize that . . ."
- good listening and response skills
- arrangement of desks in table groups

I urge beginning teachers not to ignore community-building activities even though they feel pressured with curriculum. From my journal:

> Ariane's third grade is rushing through the day. We talk after my model lesson, and she expresses amazement at how calm and measured the lesson was. She is not satisfied with the way her day begins. She makes a list of the first five things that will happen tomorrow. I suggest she try to put everything in slow motion and add a joyful activity, the choral reading of "Knitted Things" by Karla Kuskin from *Sing a Song of Popcorn* (1988). Ariane and I role play and assign clock time to each activity. The next week she reports that being more deliberate seems beneficial for students. On Tuesday, when a child asked to repeat the choral reading of "Knitted Things" before dismissal, others chimed in to indicate their pleasure in this activity.

Workers in production line factories produce more goods when they don't talk. I think the idea of "time on task" grew out of this understanding. Applied to education, it is interpreted to mean more work gets accomplished in a silent classroom, so some protégés are unsure about how much talking to tolerate. It is easy for them to feel that a quiet classroom is the most productive one. However, this overlooks what we have learned through research—that learning is enhanced by interaction among students. Again, my notebook:

> Whitney McCarthy, a first-year teacher at Coleytown School, asks if the room is too noisy. We discuss the difference between pandemonium and productive noise. I suggest that she research for a few minutes and listen to different conversational groups. She can speak quietly to children if she thinks they are too noisy or off topic. She has an expression to ask for less noise I like, "using a six-inch voice."

ROOM ARRANGEMENT

The room arrangement has a direct impact on consistency, motivation, responsibility, and the classroom community. I like to help protégés think of arranging their rooms with desks in table groups so children can talk quietly about their work. I prefer four children in each group, but sometimes class size necessitates larger ones. Table groups make transitions easier because a protégé can call table one, two, or three to line up or come to the meeting area. Again, from my notebook:

> Raisa, a fourth grade teacher in the Bronx, follows my suggestion and rearranges her classroom. But then she is unhappy with the amount of noise. We discuss teaching her class to work well in groups. The children brainstorm how a good table group would look during the reading workshop and create a reference chart to hang in the room. Next, Raisa will help the class create a rubric so individuals and groups can monitor their performance.

Where a child sits has an impact on his peer relationships. I recommend to protégés that seating be changed frequently so children get to know and work with everyone in the room. I teach how to change desks. If there are five table groups of four students, a protégé needs a deck of cards with four aces, four twos, threes, fours, and fives. He fans out the cards and lets each student choose one. All twos sit at the same table. Children with special needs can be provided for by quietly making sure they get the right card that will seat them close to the chalkboard or with a supportive friend.

Another factor in room arrangement is space for a comfortable meeting area. Older children may want to bring chairs, so space is needed to do this safely. Younger children like to sit in close proximity on the floor. They can be instructed to sit in a circle or a clump, depending on the activity. A good meeting area has either a chalkboard or chart stand close by so the protégé can write when necessary.

CLASS MEETING

Class meetings help solve problems, build responsibility, and solidify the classroom community. Readers can find more details about class meetings in *Teaching Children to Care* (Charney 1992) and *Positive Discipline* (Nelson 1987).

"Without our help," writes Ruth Charney, "children will 'solve' a problem by manufacturing an excuse, blaming someone else, or providing an empty promise to the teacher so she will shut up. But children will become involved in problem-solving if we give them help in dealing with what matters most in their lives. The episodes of the playground, the bus and the classroom have deep and immediate meanings compared to contrived work sheets, or abstractions children gather from soap operas and older siblings" (1992, pp. 75–76).

I encourage protégés to hold a class meeting once a week. Students determine the agenda by putting suggestions on a special paper that is on a clipboard next to the teacher's desk. First, the class gives compliments about behavior or work: "I like the way Mark began his story about his dog. It pulled me in." "Tim went out of his way to help Philip join the recess soccer game today." After compliments, the group discusses the next agenda item. An example about a class meeting from my notebook:

> Trisha's class is expert at tattling, and it drives her crazy. She is pleased when Laura puts tattling on the class meeting agenda. The discussion is lengthy. Some children have no clue about why this isn't appropriate behavior. One discussion is only a beginning, but Trisha can remind tattlers of the meeting when they approach her to tattle. Trisha can continue the discussion as the need arises.

Karen Wrobel, a beginning second grade teacher in Westport, has another tattling solution. A lovely, stuffed teddy bear sits on her chair. Teddy carries a sign, "Tell me. I'm all ears." When a child comes to tattle, Karen suggests he tell his story to the teddy bear instead of to the teacher. Karen continues to pay attention when children need her to listen.

REFERENCE CHARTS

Reference charts make things visible for the class community. They encourage the habit of looking things up, they are guides for work and behavior, they are sources of spelling words, and they are a record of what has happened. They can include:

- poems
- guidelines for choosing a book

- lists of writing topics
- a list of what to do when work is finished
- class rules and agreements
- standards for work and/or behavior
- rubrics
- ideas for reading response
- vocabulary words for a topic being studied
- information about books or authors

I help protégés understand that reference charts will be different from year to year. They are written by the group, not the teacher alone. They are in process and can be added to when a student has a new idea. The wording on reference charts reflects the actual words of the students. I suggest that protégés begin a reference chart as a rough draft on newsprint and later copy it on better paper before it is hung up. The draft can be a demonstration about how to edit and revise.

DISCUSSION TECHNIQUES

It is immediately obvious when a protégé knows how to lead a good discussion. Everyone in the class feels safe to contribute and risk trying out ideas. I encourage protégés to think about discussion techniques from the beginning of my work with them.

A skillful discussion leader doesn't repeat what people in the group say, but says, "Uh huh," or "Yes," or "That's an interesting idea." This forces the group to listen to the contributions of all participants rather than to listen only to the teacher. Students should be taught not to repeat but to piggyback on the ideas of others. "When Ted talked about reading the summary on the back cover, it reminded me that. . . ". Or, "Sam made me think about my favorite character when he talked about his. . . ". Good discussions have few interruptions. Children learn how important it is to respect each speaker by allowing her to finish her thoughts.

IT IS IMPORTANT FOR PROTÉGÉS TO SPEND TIME ON CLASSROOM management to make sure the happy, well-functioning classroom has all its ingredients, such as consistency, motivated students, and a strong classroom community. All teachers, beginning and experienced, can fine tune their classroom organization so that a smooth, healthy atmosphere for learning underlies its structure. Some of the things mentioned in this chapter look simple, but that is deceptive—they take practice and skill. Mentors can help protégés become more rigorous about teaching when they are critically honest and can document the conversation with specific details observed in protégés' classrooms.

ELEMENTS OF CLASSROOM MANAGEMENT AND ORGANIZATION

- consistency
- motivating students
- workshop teaching
- explicit teaching
- giving responsibility
- classroom community
- room arrangement
- class meeting
- reference charts
- discussion techniques

REFERENCES

Charney, Ruth Sidney. 1992. *Teaching Children to Care: Management in the Responsive Classroom.* Greenfield, MA: Northeast Foundation for Children.

Charney, Ruth Sidney, Marlynn K. Clayton, and Chip Wood. 1995. *The Responsive Classroom.* Greenfield, MA: Northeast Foundation for Children.

Cisneros, Sandra. 1984. *The House on Mango Street.* New York: Vintage Books.

DeRegniers, Beatrice Schenk. 1988. *Sing a Song of Popcorn, Every Child's Book of Poems.* New York: Scholastic.

Kristof, Nicholas D. 1997. *The New York Times Magazine.* (August 17) 40–44.

Kuskin, Karla. "Knitted Things." 1988. In *Sing a Song of Popcorn, Every Child's Book of Poems.* B. DeRegniers, ed. New York: Scholastic.

Nelson, Jane. 1987. *Positive Discipline.* New York: Ballantine Books.

Rylant, Cynthia. 1985. *The Relatives Came.* New York: Bradbury Press.

Wilder, Laura Ingalls. 1953. *Little House in the Big Woods.* New York: Harper & Row.

4

Knowing About Learning

*T*en years ago as a member of a teacher research group, I looked with fresh eyes at student learning. I interviewed second graders about what they thought they had learned in writing, what helped them improve as writers, and which class members they considered the best writers and why. This led me to look at my own learning so I could help my students even more. I mulled over the conditions in which I learned best, what motivated me to learn, who helped me, and the steps I needed to go through while learning. More recently, I have viewed my learning in different ways as I participated in study groups at The Reading and Writing Project. My thoughts have been directed to helping the protégés I teach in New York City, Westchester County, and in Westport.

IT HELPS PROTÉGÉS BECOME BETTER TEACHERS WHEN THEY work from the context of their own learning, so specific and detailed discussion of learning is an important ingredient of the mentor/protégé relationship. This chapter primarily focuses on protégé learning, although student learning enters the discussion because the two are congruent.

ACTIVE LEARNING IS SUPPORTED BY THE GROUP

A protégé can clearly understand that learning is supported by the group when he is participating in a peer group that is discussing classroom practices. He can see the benefits of group support firsthand. Understanding this connection should not be left to chance, but explicitly discussed in group sessions.

At the Columbus Magnet School in New Rochelle, New York, it was clear that teachers took ideas discussed in the study group and used them in their classrooms. The group began by placing samples of children's writing at each grade level as a framework for our discussions. We looked at these pieces to see what hallmarks we could discover at each age. Teachers who never taught primary grades were fascinated by how writing began in kindergarten and first grade, and teachers who never taught intermediate grades were awed by what students could learn through the years.

Once the group members had an understanding of how children wrote at different grade levels, they looked in depth at their own students to see the range of accomplishment. Then they were ready to dig deeper into the specifics of their writing workshops and question the strengths and weaknesses of their own classroom practices. From my notebook about working at Columbus Magnet School:

> Elizabeth Alexander, a fourth grade teacher, was aware that when she talked about writing in complete sentences, some children didn't follow through. She decided to do research. She asked her students the question, "What is a sentence?" Answers revealed that many were unclear about the concept and that Elizabeth needed to teach more about sentence construction. When she described this work to the group, everyone was excited. Other teachers decided to ask students questions that would provide focus for their teaching.

Columbus Magnet School teachers began to work their rooms with a new alertness to ambiguity and assumptions. They encouraged children to do as they had done—to ask questions and search for answers as they stimulated students to speculate and take risks. Some teachers reported to the group that they thought this led to more rigorous student writing. Other teachers were encouraged to look more closely at student work and nudge children as they extended the boundaries of learning.

Talk

Talk is a strong component of learning in a group. Ideas introduced by one group member may strike a chord in someone else, encouraging the exploration of new frontiers in classroom practice. In New Rochelle, the study group talk became a model for teachers to take back to their classrooms. Teachers saw the value of that talk for their learning as they continued to participate in the group year after year.

In the beginning, we set guidelines for our talk. We posted those guidelines on a reference chart as teachers would in their classrooms. As our meetings continued, talk became even more important to this community of learners as they valued the support of other staff members, and the talk generated fresh discoveries. Talk became as important to the group as sunshine and rain are to the garden.

Sometimes protégés do not understand the significance of talk and how it impacts learning. From my journal:

> Stuart is uncomfortable when the noise level begins to rise. Students didn't talk together about their work in class when he was young. I lend Stuart my book, *On Their Way, Celebrating Second Graders as They Read and Write* (Fraser and Skolnick 1994). I ask him to read the chapter on talk so we can discuss it.
>
> When Stuart and I meet to discuss the talk chapter, I can tell from the conversation that it will take a while for him to feel comfortable when the room is not silent. We plan to teach his students to have productive writing talk. For a mini-lesson, I will coach Dana to ask Josh questions about his piece, "My Little Brother." "I wonder if you can add details about how your brother acts when he sees a big dog? Tell me what he does." Next, each student will have a partner to talk about her writing. She will try to help her partner add specific details to make the piece more telling. Stuart and I will monitor the conversations so we can discuss them later.
>
> We meet after the lesson, and Stuart cautiously says he would like to work on constructive talk between my visits. He asks for other suggestions for partner work. He wants to try it and then look at the writing to see if he can detect any changes and improvements. Maybe he just wants to get me off his back, but hopefully not. Time will tell.

Each of us has a different noise tolerance. Some protégés are better than others at accepting the noise that talk generates and have more insight into how talk helps learning. Stuart will find his own level of acceptance as we continue our work.

Talk is central to critical thinking. In the beginning of the year, I coach a protégé to teach students how to talk so they can begin to have better literature group discussions. Again, my notebook:

> Six of Karen's students talk about James Marshall's *George and Martha* books (1972). They say that George and Martha are nosy and like to play tricks on each other. I ask them to justify their point by reading examples from their books. Later, I jack up the discussion by asking why they think

George and Martha are friends, in spite of the nosiness and the tricks. The conversation stops dead as the children think. I wait. Jess raises his hand. "I think they like each other because of those tricks. They enjoy them." Emily has a different response. She says they would be lonely if they didn't have each other as friends.

This lesson was designed to help Karen, a protégé, learn how to structure response so that well reasoned thinking would bring about a better understanding of literary characters. Karen and I discuss how to extend this line of questioning and decide that the next set of questions might begin with whether students would like to have George and Martha as friends, and why.

At Columbus Magnet School, Vera Rooney and Laura Chait joined the study group bringing samples of fifth grade writing. They were understandably apprehensive about state testing and wondered how our work would help or hinder their students. As time went by, Vera and Laura felt support from the group and began to try mini-lessons, topic choice, status-of-the-class, and sharing. Laura was motivated to learn more and attended The Writing Institute at Teachers College the following summer.

The stories about learners at the Columbus Magnet School demonstrate how learning is supported by the group. Teachers who may not have thought much about changing their practices in writing became interested enough to join us when they heard talk from colleagues and their principal, Leah Rukeyser. The first year we met over lunch, the second and third years we met after school. The group continued meeting to learn together and support each other when I was no longer working at their school.

ACTIVE LEARNERS CONSTRUCT MEANING AND MAKE CONNECTIONS

Protégés know from their own learning experiences that they need time to construct meaning, to make connections to their lives and to previous knowledge. Returning to the study group at Columbus Magnet School, the teachers circled back to the same topics week after week. For example, conferring was an issue that needed many tries in the classroom and many conversations in the adult group. Still, teachers did not feel satisfied with their skills. Conferring seems like the quicksand of workshop teaching, and this group wrestled with the topic frequently. From my notebook:

> Hildy Martin draws on her conferring experiences as an adult learner when she teaches second grade. Her experiences as an adult learner include study group work, demonstration lessons in her classroom, former work as an occupational therapist, and parenting. She seems to have a monitoring

device in her head as she confers with students: she is sensitive to their needs, their learning styles, and where they are as writers. She is trying to develop a keener sense of how to discover the student writer's intentions so she can challenge students to reach for the next level of learning. She keeps accurate records of each writing conference so she can refer back to previous conferences with each child. (See Chapter 3 for more information about record keeping.) Hildy reports back to the study group about her classroom work as she strives to learn even more by inviting colleagues to critique her work.

Making personal connections can help protégés see the value of using those connections in their teaching. We can also teach from our own reading and writing experiences. From my notebook:

In Eileen's fifth grade class, I select the story "Hairs" for a mini-lesson to demonstrate how a writer can highlight one specific thing (Cisneros 1984). I tell Eileen and her class that I chose this story because my family often made remarks about my hair when I was a child. Joshua says that happens in his family, and he is going to write about hair today. Zuleka echoes his comments. Andy decides to write a story focused on jeans. This trio of pieces makes a lively writers' share session.

In a teacher workshop, I may demonstrate reading/writing connections. Charts provide a model for protégés to use in their own classrooms. Here are the beginnings of two reference charts:

HOW I WRITE WHEN I READ

- written response to literature
- savoring language to use in my own writing
- examining writers' strategies
- making notes of what I want to remember

HOW I READ WHEN I WRITE

- rereading to see where I stopped
- sharing with someone
- reading as a critic to make sure it says what I want—editing and revising
- doing research to support my writing

The group that made these charts had a provocative discussion about reading/writing connections as protégés shared their ideas.

Thinking Made Public

A good strategy for mentors to teach protégés is to make their thinking public so students can see how adults construct meaning and make connections. I model this in discussions with protégés and in the classroom. From my notebook:

> Tim is a quick study—this mini-lesson follows our discussion in which I modeled thinking aloud. Rather than plunging right into the reading, Tim takes his time with a new read aloud book. He tells the class he wants to share his process for choosing this book. He says, "This is what I thought. Let's see what this book is about. I wonder if the class will like it." Tim reads the title and the author. "Oh, I like books by Jean Fritz. What does it say on the back cover." Tim reads the back cover aloud. "Hmm, about her childhood in China. That sounds interesting because we're studying China. I'll read it at home and if I like it, then I'll try it in class" (1982).

Tim and I discuss how he can continue thinking aloud as he reads the book. I encourage him to be explicit about connections between the book and the social studies unit on China because he cannot assume that children will automatically build those bridges.

Prior Knowledge

Prior knowledge helps protégés make connections between teaching and their own lives. A mentor is well-advised to probe and listen carefully to a new protégé's previous experiences. These experiences are the rich soil in which the effective mentoring experience is to be grown. From my notebook:

> Gail comes to our mentoring relationship with years of teaching experience. She becomes interested in learning more about nonfiction reading strategies when her supervisor suggests that new ideas might help her students in standardized testing. Gail and I discuss her experiences with nonfiction reading. She knows a lot about how to look through text, how to read section headings, how to bring her prior knowledge to her reading, and how to take notes. We discuss what she already knows that can help students and what I can do to supplement her repertoire.

Flexible Grouping

Protégés often find it easier to teach to the whole class, and my job may be to assist them in managing the room when students are not moving in lock step. An easy place to begin is in writing workshop where students are so interested in their work that the teacher can easily handle a situation when everyone is not doing the same thing at the same time. Here are two stories about Sandy:

> I coach Sandy to teach her class about having better writing conferences. She teaches several role-playing mini-lessons as the class talks about conferring strategies that help writers. Today she is looking for new ways to facilitate student conferences. There is a sign-up sheet on a clipboard for children who are ready to confer. She asks her class for suggestions about how they can discover who is willing to interrupt their own work to confer with a classmate. A student remarks that they can look at the clipboard, then seek the next person on the list, so conferring partners can be easily established as Sandy continues her work.

> Sandy has a group of students who are ready to revise, edit, and publish. She wants them to do other writing activities until she is ready to help everyone begin publishing. We talk about pulling out a small group and working with them while other students continue to write and have peer conferences. Although Sandy is uneasy about this, I convince her to try because there will be two of us in the room when she begins. The week after she works with a group teaching revision strategies, she discovers that other students already know a lot about the process. They have been listening as she worked with the first group. Getting a second small group of students started is much easier.

Flexible grouping is easy to demonstrate in adult workshops. The strategy of turning to the person sitting next to you and then sharing with the whole group is often used to help construct meaning. Partners and small groups can discuss different professional articles before they are shared and discussed by the entire group. Asking teachers to change where they sit and to work with new people in teacher workshops helps protégés see firsthand the value of flexible grouping.

Diversified Teaching Strategies

The construction of meaning is supported with the use of diversified teaching strategies. I try to demonstrate a variety of strategies both in model lessons and in teacher workshops. These strategies may include:

- jotting—each person quickly writes her ideas before sharing with the group
- working with a partner or small group
- using the whip—going quickly around the circle, everyone sharing a sentence or two in response to a question

- using reference charts—ideas for work or behavior, standards, rubrics written by the group and hung in the room
- working the room—what the teacher does during reading or writing workshop
- teaching from student information or comments
- role playing—a dramatic demonstration designed to help solve a problem

These strategies are designed to help protégés diversify their teaching practices because each group of learners contains students who have different interests and learning styles. After I model one of these strategies, I may ask a protégé to try it out followed by a discussion of how it went.

LEARNERS ARE MOTIVATED BY INTEREST AND EMOTION

Protégés volunteer to learn new teaching strategies when interest is created or their curiosity is aroused. A protégé can be a beginning teacher or one transferred to a new grade. Perhaps he gets pulled in by another staff member, or has heard a convincing speaker at a professional meeting. The protégé will continue learning when there is just enough challenge to keep him interested and the mentoring relationship fits him just like a comfortable old shoe.

At the Columbus Magnet School, interest was created through the drumbeat of teacher talk and the principal's skill in hiring and then encouraging teachers to learn new teaching strategies. Then it was my job to make the study group rigorous and exciting enough so teachers were willing to attend. I listened carefully to what members said and made time to grapple with the questions that grew from the thinking and interests of the group.

When I ask a study group to read an article, I know it may be lost in a pile of papers on their desks. So I tried a different strategy with a group in Westport by trying to tap into their interests and prior knowledge. I asked teachers to bring a professional article about reading to share the following week. Each protégé was expected to summarize his article so the group could discuss it. Not everyone brought an article, of course, but there was still a great variety of articles and the group discussion was excellent.

In her book *Emotion: The On/Off Switch for Learning,* Priscilla Vail demonstrates how confidence, anger, friendship, and anxiety influence the learning process. An emotional response either blocks higher level thinking or opens up that ability. This is, of course, true for protégés and their learning. They need to feel successful and respected as they decide how they will follow through on suggestions made by mentors or a support group.

LEARNERS HAVE THEIR OWN LEARNING TIMETABLE AND MAY NOT DEMONSTRATE THEIR LEARNING IMMEDIATELY

Unless a protégé is explicit in the discussion of her learning, a mentor cannot always be sure what new ideas are being assimilated. I may come to the end of a mentoring relationship and be unclear about what has been accomplished. But I have learned that some ideas will not be absorbed until a future time. I may need to be satisfied with little things, such as a comment, a smile, a willingness to meet.

Protégés make learning more visible when they share their notebooks with a mentor or a group of colleagues. We get other glimpses into learning by observing a protégé teach. A protégé can remove the protective covering from her learning if she is willing to make her thinking, writing, and actions more public.

Here's a story from my notebook:

> After a discussion in the study group at Columbus Magnet School, Janet Waller returns to her class and asks students what they are learning about how to become better writers. She reports to her colleagues that her students join this discussion easily. Most of them can say exactly what they think is helping them learn more about writing. Janet reviews several interviews for the group, using her notes.

Leslie Hart points out the idiosyncratic nature of learning in *Human Brain and Human Learning.* ". . . a teacher aggressively instructing a class of twenty-five is actually *not* addressing a group at all, but rather twenty-five individual brains each of which will attend to what it chooses . . ." (p. 78). This is true for our work with protégés individually and in groups. We cannot assume that each protégé is hearing the same thing or will act similarly when trying out a new strategy.

I assume that when I teach a lesson in a different way, I will teach it to a new set of students. An example from my notebook:

> When I pull out *Goodnight Moon* (Brown 1975), the third graders in Debbie's class are very excited. They know and love this book. I read the book and allow children to share a few memories or comments. Then I ask what the rabbit is doing as he says goodnight. Andy says that he is saying goodnight to all the things around him. From Andy's remark I segue into my lesson—reading the room for writing ideas. Some students are interested in reading the room for the first time. A few focus on the classroom,

some on a room at home. This has not happened before even though I had previously talked about reading the room.

The Pace of Learning

Each protégé will learn at her own pace. While we are not always in the position of being able to wait for a protégé to come to us, when we can and they do, special things can develop. In my Westport work, I have the luxury of the whole school year. From my notebook:

> Pam Syndercombe did her student teaching with two pros in Westport—Donna Skolnick and Caltha Crowe. She is familiar with the student and parent community, other staff members, and school routines as she begins her first year of teaching. Most of all, she needs to be reassured that everything is going well. She isn't ready for demonstration lessons until she gets her feet on the ground and tries things out for herself. In January Pam asks for help with writing workshop and strategies for dealing with some of the more troublesome students in her class.

A skillful mentor gets to know the protégé to discover what he is ready to learn because the mentor knows that learning does not occur in any prescribed progression. There is no list of skills that must be learned in a specific order. There is no cookbook for our work. Again, from my notebook:

> Rose found me in the hall the second year I worked at her school in the Bronx. "I wanted you to know, Jane," she said, "that I am using wait time. You talked about it last year, but I guess I wasn't ready to use it until now. Realizing this has helped me understand what you meant when you talked about how each learner has his own timetable. I am learning how wait time helps children find their voices and do more in-depth thinking during discussions."

LEARNERS ARE REWARDED BY THEIR EFFORTS

Protégés know from personal experience that learning brings its own rewards. These rewards may come from:

- a class session where a new strategy works well
- an administrator who gives a favorable evaluation
- students who demonstrate positive attitudes toward learning and school

- children who demonstrate their learning in new and unpredictable ways
- a group of colleagues who show interest in the protégé's ideas

This is from my notebook:

> Susan looks at me in surprise. "I hadn't thought of that before," she says. "I didn't realize how important it would be for me to keep a writer's notebook so I could talk about it with students." As Susan begins to keep her own notebook, her conversations with students take a different tone. She speaks with authority and self-knowledge. Susan remarks about the newfound power she feels as a writing teacher.

A protégé may need to await the beginning of the new school year before she can appreciate what she has learned, as Whitney McCarthy did:

> Whitney speaks about starting her second year of teaching. She says, "I wish I'd known how much better it would be. I have things in the file, for example, for Thanksgiving, I don't have to make everything up. I feel more comfortable at staff meetings and with parents. I feel I can share at grade level meetings, but most of all, I feel so much more at home with my students . . . I'm just having so much more fun."

IN THE SUNDAY *NEW YORK TIMES BOOK REVIEW* OF SEPTEMBER 7, 1997 (p. 27), Jonty Driver says, "The huge difficulty with learning is that it doesn't happen in straight lines; it progresses by leaps, or sometimes meanders around on a plateau and then sprints for a precipice (up or down)." As protégés reflect on their own learning, we can help them recognize its uneven nature and how to make use of this insight in their classrooms. Knowing more about learning will assist them to structure their teaching to accommodate the needs of the younger learners in their classrooms.

ACTIVE LEARNERS

- can be supported by a group
- construct meaning and make connections
- are motivated by interest and emotion
- have their own learning timetable and may not demonstrate learning immediately
- receive intrinsic reward for their efforts

REFERENCES

Brown, Margaret Wise. 1975. *Goodnight Moon.* New York: Harper & Row.

Cisneros, Sandra. 1984. *The House on Mango Street.* New York: Vintage Books.

Driver, Jonty. "Understanding Understanding." *The New York Times, Sunday Book Review.* September 7, 1997: 27.

Fraser, Jane and Donna Skolnick. 1994. *On Their Way, Celebrating Second Graders as They Read and Write.* Portsmouth, N.H.: Heinemann.

Fritz, Jean. 1982. *Homesick, My Own Story.* New York: Putnam.

Hart, Leslie A. 1983. *Human Brain and Human Learning.* Oak Cress, AZ: Books for Educators.

Marshall, James. 1972. *George and Martha.* Boston: Houghton Mifflin.

Vail, Priscilla. 1994. *Emotion: The On/Off Switch for Learning.* Rosemont, NJ: Modern Learning Press.

5

Reflect to Learn

*T*he border of perennial plants in front of my house is one of my favorite parts of the garden. Plants poke faithfully through the cool earth each spring after I clear away the mulch. Each plant begins to grow according to its own timetable—the astilbe, purple columbine, shasta daisies, lavender, coneflowers, peonies, and pulmunaria. I may add a new plant to increase variety and color, to lengthen the blooming season, or to attract more hummingbirds.

PERENNIALS RETURN YEAR AFTER YEAR. WHILE MOST OF MY relationships with protégés are not perennial, I trust the impact of our work will mean that tender shoots show each fall and grow to lush blossoms as the year progresses. The important part of this work is what lasts and what is used as a stepping-stone to a new strategy.

Reflection is the fulcrum of learning that lasts. Without it, I doubt if protégés could sustain the changes we attempt to implement. Reflection provides distance so a protégé can look back at what has happened. The word *reflection* brings a mirror to mind. When we hold up a mirror, we can examine images in detail. Without it, we could have a distorted view or no view at all.

A big leap in my understanding of the need for reflection occurred when I first participated in a teacher research group. As I learned alongside my students, observing and taking notes in my journal, I realized how much they had to teach me. My journal became like a large mirror that stood in the middle of Room 13. I used it to help me reflect on the needs of my students and what was happening in the classroom. These reflective images made it possible to implement what I was learning from my students. They encouraged me to give them more responsibility for decision making and more choice to students' reading and writing activities.

Reflection depends on assessment and evaluation as a door depends on the hinge to the door jamb. All three, assessment, evaluation, and reflection need to be embedded in the relationship between mentor and protégé. My job with protégés has been to help them engage in assessment and evaluation as they learn to scrutinize themselves as both learners and practitioners.

PROTÉGÉ LEARNING
GROUNDED REFLECTION

At the Columbus Magnet School in New Rochelle, New York, Hildy Martin and Janet Waller are teachers who are continuously engaged in reflection as they strive to refine their classroom practices. These women probed and analyzed what I demonstrated in their classrooms; they analyzed what they did between my visits. They looked at the content of lessons, they examined the reactions of students, they watched to see what carryover occurred to other curriculum areas. When I no longer worked in their classrooms, they continued the search as they refined their repertoires based on their analysis of the strengths, weaknesses, and learning styles of individual students. They modified their own actions based upon that analysis. Janet and Hildy continue learning as they take advantage of professional opportunities that are available, such as calendar days, Saturday reunions, and study groups offered by The Reading and Writing Project. They teach and attend inservice sessions in their district. Their approach is an aggressive learning stance designed to make them even better teachers than they already are. They want to bring the best to their students.

By the second and third years at Columbus Magnet School, Janet and Hildy continued to play an active role in the study group that met after school. This group continued to meet after my visits were over as the teachers experienced the power of learning and reflecting in a group.

Some protégés seem naturally reflective, others need coaching and encouragement. Some are more comfortable working alone, while others clearly like the support of a group. A mentor needs to provide for both styles when working in a school. My notebook again:

> I am trying to help Todd build deliberate thinking into his teaching framework and become a reflective practitioner. We talk about what happened when Robin interrupted my mini-lesson to say she didn't understand, and Sam was upset because he wanted to read his piece during the share

time. My question to Todd at the end of our conference is this: Would he have reflected on these incidents and acted on them if I had not been there?

An example of reflecting in a group, from my notebook:

Liz was transferred from the sixth grade to the fourth. She asks the group for help because she isn't sure how to teach about writing strong paragraphs for research reports. Myrna suggests that Liz model writing on chart paper and offers to give Liz the paper she needs. I add the strategy of looking at some good nonfiction writing. Liz can photocopy some pages so her students can analyze how a paragraph is constructed.

Why Reflect?

Let's return to the story about Todd. The reason to think about individual students is so that Todd and I can hone our teaching to help students. Knowing individual children well and having a deeper understanding of them as learners is a focal point for teaching in reading and writing workshop.

It helped me when Robin interrupted in frustration to say that she didn't understand. She let me know I had to do a better job explaining the kernel of the mini-lesson. I needed to go back, rephrase, and write on chart paper so that every child would have a clearer view. We don't always have Robins who are willing to express their confusion, so I may model asking children to repeat directions. What will they do first, second, and so on. And, I may ask students to explain *why* they are doing something.

Todd and I talked about Sam's frustration when he was not one of the two children chosen to share. I have seen protégés bend and extend share time to pacify a child like Sam. On this occasion, it was clear that children had been sitting for as long as they could. I tried to help Sam feel better by talking to him privately as Todd began to organize the next activity. I reassured him that Todd and I kept track of who had turns to share, and because there was no check mark next to his name on the list, he might share next time. But I reported to Todd that I didn't promise—you can never be sure what might interfere, and I wouldn't want to disappoint Sam again.

Record Keeping

I showed Todd what I wrote in my notebook as this lesson progressed. There were notes about Robin and Sam together with observations about other children. On the opposite page, as Todd and I talked, I made reflective notes, asked myself questions, and did preliminary planning. This double entry format is the most informative record keeping I know how to do. (See Chapter 2 for additional discussion of double entry journals.)

I kept a loose leaf binder when I first began teaching. It had a section for each child in the class. Sometimes I encourage protégés to try this kind of notebook, using mailing labels to stick down in the sections of the notebook for individual children. From my notebook:

> This week I am surprised when I visit in Hildy's class. She is no longer using mailing labels. She says they became too cumbersome for her, that she never found time to transfer them into the notebook. She is trying something different. She has photocopied pages that have a grid, six high by four wide. Each space has a child's name. At the top of the page it says Week of _____ and Lesson _____. She has them on a clipboard. Hildy acknowledges that she has to flip through all the pages when she wants to find information about one child, but it helps her track who she sees during one week to make sure she confers with everyone.
>
> Mara Schwartz, at Coleytown School, has a file box. She writes her observations on 3″ x 5″ index cards that she carries around. She has a bunch of them in her hand as she confers with students. A different way to use index cards is to tape 4″ x 6″ cards to a clipboard, graduated so that the names of the children show on the bottom. Then the cards can be flipped up to expose the one a protégé is ready to use.

Whatever record keeping system a protégé chooses to use, it is important to be consistent and regular so she has observations for reflection and planning and has meaningful things to say to a parent who comes to talk about a child's progress.

The Feedback Loop

Students need feedback during the course of their learning, whether they are seven, seventeen, twenty-seven, or seventy. I remember Ben, a second grader, who told my colleague Donna Skolnick, when she praised him, that he wanted to know what he did well so that he could do it again. Ben was able to verbalize his need for feedback. He helped us have a real learning experience when he made us keenly aware of the importance of providing feedback to all students. I try to remember Ben when working with adult learners.

Feedback from a mentor helps protégés assess and evaluate their own learning and behavior. This feedback should be specific and supportive combined with constructive criticism. I may say, "It helped the class when you explained what Robert was doing in his response journal. Have you considered writing a reference chart about ideas for writing a reader's response?"

Another notebook entry:

Judy, a fourth grade teacher, is working hard to learn about teaching the reading workshop. Our discussions are frequent, long, and analytical. Judy deserves an extra pat on the back. In addition to the usual feedback, I ask if she is interested in attending the Summer Institute at Teachers College. When her response is positive, we agree that I will inquire if it is possible to have her attendance supported financially by her school district.

There is no road map highlighted with a single route to follow for the progressive classroom. That is why feedback from an empathetic mentor is an important component of the mentor/protégé work.

REFLECTION HELPS CREATE GOOD TEACHING

Yetta Goodman said that "the evaluation of the students becomes an evaluation of ourselves and of the curriculum" (1989, p. 3). Protégés can be encouraged to use both assessment and evaluation to modify their actions and teaching strategies to benefit children. What is the difference between assessment and evaluation? According to Regie Routman, "Assessment refers to data collection and the gathering of evidence. Evaluation implies bringing meaning to that data through interpretation, analysis, and reflection and includes the kinds of instructional decisions that are made by careful examination of the evidence" (1991, p. 302).

About assessment and evaluation from my notebook:

> Sarah uses both assessment and evaluation to make her plans. After I teach a mini-lesson about recommending books to classmates, Sarah and I discuss what to do next. We have recorded what students said in the circle. Sarah wants to continue this theme tomorrow. She decides to summarize the circle comments and model for the class by verbalizing how she would recommend the current read aloud to another teacher. She will echo the circle comments and attribute them to appropriate students.

Another notebook entry:

> Lesa Tischler, at Coleytown School, combines assessment with evaluation. She remarks that following a demonstration lesson she writes down the content of the lesson and her observations about what happened. She feels she can learn more when she uses the expertise of others as a basis for reflection so she can repeat or draw upon the lesson again, this year or next.

Protégés can reflect on some of the following things as they consider their teaching:

- student behavior
- student writing
- classroom relationships
- questions children ask
- records of participation in readers' and writers' share
- book choices
- responses to literature
- information from parents

The reason for assessment and evaluation is to roll back the boundaries of learning. In *Assessment, Continuous Learning,* Lois Bridges says, "Assessment separate from instruction is of little value." She continues, "When we evaluate our students' learning or ask them to evaluate themselves, our primary goal should be to help them learn more" (1995, pp. 25–26). In a mentor's work, the protégés are our students. Our job is to encourage their reflection so they learn more about their teaching. My notebook:

> "How'd I do?" Whitney McCarthy, at Coleytown School, asks after I observe a first grade reading group. We discuss the positives: her voice, how she phrases questions, how she picks up on little clues, the progress students are making, the attentiveness of children. I suggest she consider varying her technique of calling on children. It is a good idea not to always go in order around the table. Some children try to anticipate what they will be asked to read. If they are busy figuring that out, they cannot pay attention to what is happening in the group. We discuss the idea that if we have children reading in a group, we want to make it worthwhile for each child.

Whitney seeks my feedback because she is constantly asking herself how she is doing with the intent of modifying and improving her teaching. Reflection is entwined in our work as we look at what worked, what didn't work, and how to change things so they will be better for her students.

My notebook, again:

> Nan and I debrief following the mini-lesson about searching for a seed— a small phrase or idea to expand into a new piece of writing—in the writer's notebook. The class set to work quickly and purposely, except for Amanda and Ronald who don't seem to grasp the concept. They use the writing time

to make new notebook entries. Nan remarks that they are very literal and the seed metaphor is probably unintelligible to them even though I also explained it in concrete terms. We plan what Nan can do tomorrow and in the intervening days until I return with a view toward helping the whole class, including Amanda and Ronald.

Nan and I immediately observed that two students were having difficulty with a new concept we had introduced. Closer observation might reveal that more children needed help to implement the concept of using their notebooks as a source for an idea that matters enough to them that they would work on it over time.

Nan and I knew we would continue to revise our teaching based on observation and reflection about students and ourselves. We were engaged in a process Lois Bridges described in her article, "The Art of Teaching Evaluation and Revision," in *The Whole Language Evaluation Book* (1989, p. 15). She said, "Good teaching, like good writing, is created and crafted through a continual process of revision."

TEACHING REFLECTION TO STUDENTS AND PROTÉGÉS

We can become role models for students when we question ourselves and make those questions public. My notebook:

> Jim, a fifth grade teacher, models reflection for his class. At the beginning of his mini-lesson he states what he is going to do. "I am thinking aloud so you can hear how I reflect on my teaching. I know I learn more when I ask myself questions such as, "How am I going to do this? Why am I doing this work? How can I do a better job?" He verbalizes his thoughts about yesterday's mini-lesson. "I wonder if everyone understands why we're keeping writer's notebooks?" He goes on. Before he finishes the mini-lesson, the class constructs a reference chart, "Questions We Can Ask Ourselves About Our Learning."

How Am I Doing?

As I lead teacher workshops, I take notes so I can reflect and plan for the next gathering. I ask myself, "How am I doing?" I also pose that question to participants and give them a chance to ask questions. I try to show them how I use reflection as I teach. It is the same when we teach students of any age.

In the November 1997 issue of *Primary Voices K–6,* Jane Hansen says, "Many students . . . need periodic stopping points along the way to reflect on what they've done, what they're in the middle of, and where they are going."

This is certainly true for protégés. I try to build periodic stopping points into our work.

From my notebook:

> I talk with Andrea Lippel at Columbus Magnet School after the first time I work in her third grade class. I ask if she thinks I was on target with my mini-lesson about keeping notebooks. Does she think the children understood? Will she be able to follow through until my next visit? Andrea observed the lesson and knows her students well. With my questions, I try to model how a colleague can help me reflect on my teaching.

Lucky teachers have colleagues with whom they reflect about teaching. Critical Friend is a term used by Arthur L. Costa and Bena Kallick in *Assessment in the Learning Organization, Shifting the Paradigm* (ASCD, 1995). "In staff development, teachers use this Critical Friends strategy to plan and reflect on their process . . . . this strategy allows them to understand one another's work at a deeper level" (1995, p. 155). The Critical Friend concept can be formalized to include the use of scoring rubrics as a Critical Friend tries to "provide feedback that will stretch the work to its best potential" (p. 155) (see Chapter 8).

I think of myself as a critical friend in my relationship with protégés. My job is to:

- encourage close observation of students
- observe and expand teaching strategies used by protégés
- encourage reflection
- push the learning of protégés and students
- demonstrate explicit, active teaching
- model record keeping systems

ASSESSMENT AND EVALUATION OF PROTÉGÉS

The relationship between the mentor and her protégés needs to be honest and confidential. I bear in mind the Critical Friend concept as I try to stretch learning by being both critical and supportive. Fortunately, I am not involved in any evaluation of protégés that impacts on rehiring. Criticism I have for a protégé is designed to be constructive, is specific, is based on evidence, and is strictly confidential. Some protégés can be their own harshest critics, and then I try to soften things. My notebook, again:

Ron teaches a mini-lesson designed to encourage some recalcitrant boys to participate in class. After the lesson, he surprises me when he says he couldn't detect any change that day. I try to put this in perspective by saying it will probably take a series of lessons plus his personal encouragement to break up this group and help the boys feel that it is OK to share their thinking with the group. My job is to help Ron see that attitudes built up over days, months, or years are not changed by one mini-lesson.

Another example from my notebook:

Sue is a beginning teacher. I cannot determine if she is engaged in self-assessment because she is consumed with class control, supervisory evaluations, and passing the state exam for new teachers. We talk about this. I try to be gentle, and Sue accepts my comments because, I think, she is basically a very reflective person. She has neglected this part of her learning because of all the pressures.

I guide the conversation to talk about how reflection can help in her very real concerns, especially class control and supervision. I detail how reflection about class control and improving her skills in management will impact what a supervisor observes. We decide to look at the behavior of a few troublesome students and devise strategies to moderate their behavior. Sue knows that this will benefit the entire classroom community.

THE POWER OF A GROUP

It can be a sticky wicket to help a protégé toward reflection if she is not naturally inclined to be reflective. Sometimes being part of a group is a helpful way to nudge protégés. A story from my notebook:

I work hard with Jean over a period of weeks, but she depends on me to analyze and reflect as she waits for me to institute changes in her reading classroom. I invite her to join a group of teachers in the building who are meeting twice a month to discuss the teaching of reading.

After attending a few of these meetings, Jean comments about how analytical the others are. She wonders if they are too self-critical. This opens up an interesting discussion as we talk again about how reflection can guide her teaching. I urge her to keep a journal or notebook.

Jean continues to meet with her colleagues, and I can begin to see small movement. The group convinces her that recording in journals is critical to their teaching. The power of the group helps her begin to tap into new ways to reflect on her teaching day. She starts to record the comments of her students as they talk about reading. We analyze these comments together and use them as a base for planning mini-lessons.

WE CAN ASSIST PROTÉGÉS IN LOOKING BACK TO DISCOVER what did and didn't work in their classrooms. The discovery may come from a notebook with kidwatching records. It may result from the examination of student work. It may follow a conversation with a mentor. The purpose of the reflection is to find the path with an open view ahead, pointing toward further refinement of the protégé's repertoire. The protégé may need to go back to review her repertoire in order to replant some strategies in richer soil. She may wish to throw away something that is withering and replace it with a fresher idea. Or, she may decide to add a new strategy. Whatever the reason and whatever the action that follows, the job of the mentor is to be a Critical Friend who supports and encourages reflection that will result in learning and growth.

REFLECTIVE PRACTICE

- Learning is grounded in reflection.
- Reflection leads to better teaching.
- Reflection can be modeled for students.
- Mentors can model reflection for protégés.
- Mentors can help protégés with self-assessment and evaluation.
- Reflection may be encouraged by a peer group.

REFERENCES

Bridges, Lois. 1995. *Assessment, Continuous Learning.* Los Angeles, CA: The Galef Institute/ York: ME. Stenhouse Publishers.

Costa, Arthur L. and Bena Kallick, eds. 1995. *Assessment in the Learning Organization, Shifting the Paradigm.* Alexandria, VA: Association for Supervision and Curriculum Development.

Goodman, Kenneth S., Yetta M. Goodman and Wendy J. Hood. 1989. *The Whole Language Evaluation Book.* Portsmouth, NH: Heinemann.

Hansen, Jane. 1997. "Teacher Researchers Evaluate Themselves." *Primary Voices K–6.* 5 (4): 30.

Routman, Regie. 1991. *Invitations, Changing as Teachers and Learners K–12.* Portsmouth, NH: Heinemann.

6

The Parent Connection

*T*his afternoon at the Westport Public Library, I met Dan Kail. He is the father of three daughters, two of whom I taught in first grade in the late 1960s. We talked about his children, grandchildren, and the new construction at the Library. After all these years, we still feel connected. Our relationship has a perennial quality—it is renewed when we happen to meet.

COMMUNICATIONS AMONG TEACHER, STUDENT, AND HOME are like a Venn diagram where each of the three parts intersects to teach, reinforce, assess, and evaluate the other segments. The members in each segment have the responsibility to communicate with the other two groups. This chapter contains strategies and suggestions for helping protégés build and strengthen their relationships with parents. It is based on my experience with parents in the suburbs, both when I had my own classroom and my subsequent work as a retired teacher mentor. The topic of parents has seldom come up in New York City and Westchester County, New York, and then only tangentially to other discussions.

New teachers may worry about or feel threatened by the parent community. Suburban parents have a reputation of being active on behalf of their children. Parents are frequently in the school building—to pick up their children, volunteer in the school library or a classroom, attend an assembly, see the principal or a teacher. When not at school, they may be on the telephone from their office or home. The bottom line is that these parents want the very best for their children.

There is no grace period for protégés with respect to the parent community—nothing akin to driver's education for beginning drivers. The parental connection begins in a rush with new teachers speeding down the highway in heavy traffic. When Meredith was a new teacher in Westport, her principal felt uneasy about her being a beginner, even though she had a master's degree from one of the finest schools in the country. The principal asked Meredith not to tell parents that she had no prior teaching experience. This put her in a difficult position. Parents asked all kinds of questions, trying to figure out what she had done before coming to town, because she obviously was not twenty-two.

Meredith knew it was as important to build positive relationships with parents as it was to construct them with children. She recognized that parents can support or sabotage depending upon how they feel about a new teacher. This situation created a tension that Meredith and I needed to grapple with and discuss. She needed support from me because she was in a sticky situation. As her mentor, I wanted to help her drive safely to her destination.

LETTER TO PARENTS

Parents can pass along a lot of information about their children, so it is wise when protégés include them in the loop at the beginning of the year by seeking their views. I encourage protégés to send home a letter asking parents to share their observations, hopes, and dreams for their child. This letter, sent the first or second week of school, includes the following questions:

- What would you like me to know about your child?
- How does your child spend time on his own at home?
- What are your goals and expectations for your child this year?

Responses to these questions may provide in-depth, personal information for the protégé to consider. Some parents write painfully honest and confidential replies. When this happens, a letter can have a truly unique view that might not otherwise be visible.

NOTES

If a protégé's school has voice mail and/or E-mail, she can encourage parents to continue the dialogue throughout the year. Protégés should pay careful attention to how they respond to notes from parents. Notes run the gamut from asking about bringing cupcakes on a child's birthday, to parents going away and leaving their children with a sitter, to serious illness in the family. My notebook:

Walter receives a note from Susan's mother saying that Susan is complaining about the way her classmates are treating her on the playground. Walter is apprehensive because he has seen Susan be aggressive with peers. We talk it over. Walter decides to request that Susan's mother come to school for a conference. He and I role-play to help him find the words he wants to use when he talks with Susan's mom.

Unsolicited notes can go home from school when something significant has happened. If Susan, in the story above, has tried hard to modify her behavior following the conference, it would be judicious for Walter to send a short note citing specific examples of her improved behavior. This is reinforcing for Susan while it helps Walter build a positive relationship with Susan's parents. A protégé who is a good observer of children will find countless opportunities for writing positive notes to parents.

Another type of story from my notebook:

Life is changing. A protégé received an offensive note from a parent. The protégé has encouraged students to borrow books and take them home to read. One parent returned a book with a note saying that she took exception to some of its language. The parent marked this so-called offensive language in the book with a highlighter. The protégé was careful to temper her response. She talked with me, with colleagues, and her administrator before she answered the note.

The actions of this parent were inappropriate. It would have been better if she had discussed the matter with the teacher. Fortunately, the protégé had bought herself some time, and she had the backing of her administrator. The parent was asked to replace the book that belonged to the protégé, but it was an unpleasant and surprising introduction for a teacher new to the district.

PHONE CALLS

Phone calls are easy to make and they pay dividends. I coach protégés to consider making quick and frequent calls to parents. If a protégé notices a student trying something new in her writing, a quick call will tune in the family and serve as an opening for the parent and the child to talk about it over dinner. A protégé can make a telephone call to the parents when a child does something special to help—a classmate, the teacher, or someone in the school. Often a protégé only needs to leave a message on an answering machine for a busy parent.

I remember when a telephone call sometimes promoted a negative response—what did my child do wrong? How much better it is to call for positive reasons, to single out a risk-taking experience or a learning break-through. What parent would not be pleased with such a call?

NEWSLETTERS

There are two kinds of class newsletters for protégés to consider. One is the newsletter written by the class. In second grade, we wrote a weekly edition of Room 13 News. Figure 6.1 shows the format we used. It was a reading/writing activity. Each child received a copy and illustrated it before taking it home. The content varied, but could have been about:

- learning a new poem or song
- finishing a read aloud
- an event with another class
- taking a class trip
- an assembly
- a special visitor to class
- a cooking activity
- starting or completing a unit of study
- learning a math game
- a science activity

Many teachers write a weekly newsletter. When protégés do this they can include specific items such as the names of read alouds, books that are being read by students, news about writing workshop, math and science activities. A newsletter can quote student responses when a read aloud is finished or tell about upcoming events. Newsletters help students talk with their families about the details of their week in school.

A variation to the teacher newsletter is to provide time for students to write letters to their parents about the week. The protégé can structure these letters by reviewing events and making a list for reference before students compose their letters. The review can include mini-lessons, names of guests, or something about a read aloud. A whip, where everyone responds briefly, can answer a question such as "What did your response group discuss this week?" Another strategy would be to ask each child to jot down three things to include in the letter, then share with a partner or the table group before writing. This helps everyone think of fresh ideas. (See also the section about student rehearsal for talk in this chapter.)

ROOM 13 NEWS

Figure 6.1: Format of a weekly newsletter

BACK-TO-SCHOOL NIGHT

The pressure of the parental connection, like rush hour on the interstate, continues as Back-to-School Night approaches. It helps protégés when their colleagues talk over the format and content of that evening because each school has its own unique customs for Back-to-School Night.

I coach protégés to write out and rehearse their talk so it fits like a comfortable pair of jeans. A rehearsal helps them figure out how long they can talk and still provide time for parents to ask questions at the end. Back-to-School Night is not a time for discussion about individual children. If a parent tries to engage in talk about his child, the protégé should know it is appropriate to ask him to call the next day for an appointment.

Protégés can take note of who was unable to attend Back-to-School Night and make follow-up telephone calls to ask if these parents have questions they would like answered. This courtesy boosts the relationship between the protégé and the family. Sometimes lack of attendance is involuntary and a phone call is appreciated.

When a protégé has students write individual letters to leave on their desks for their parents, the letters need to be as well constructed as they can be, given the age and development of the children. Of course, they will not be perfect, so the protégé can use them as a talking point for her philosophy about writing and spelling.

It is important to have student work displayed on Back-to-School Night. I like the way Cathryn Kibby, Whitney McCarthy, and Kate Sanderson display writing at Coleytown School. I jotted down the following in my notebook:

> Cathryn, Whitney, and Kate are developing how they display student writing. They know first grade pieces will not be perfect, they are works in progress. The teachers write an explanation of the process involved or the teacher provides a rubric developed by the class and puts it on the wall alongside the student writing. In November, outside Whitney's classroom it said:
> To publish—your piece must have . . .

- capitals and periods
- lower case letters
- EVERY word must have a vowel
- your best writing
- a great picture

PARENT CONFERENCES

The first eight weeks of school are packed. As the protégé navigates through a myriad of meetings and new responsibilities, it is easy to feel as though he's driving in rush hour. By November, the traffic thickens even more and the pressure on the interstate heightens as the protégé speeds toward conference week. Autumn events include starting school, getting to know each student and his family, Back-to-School Night, setting professional goals, visits from supervisors, trying to learn new curriculum, establishing a classroom community—and then suddenly it is time for conferences.

Preparation for Conferences

Thorough preparation for conferences is important. Frequent observations and note taking allow a protégé to make specific comments to parents. (There are sections on record keeping in Chapters 2 and 5.) Some teachers have special forms they use for conference notes. Figure 6.2 is a sample form for making conference notes the teachers at Coleytown School share with protégés who are preparing for their first conference week in November.

It helps protégés when they engage in active listening during the fall conferences. Important information may be shared between parent and teacher that can have an impact on the child's ability to function well in school. When discussing how a student performs, there are positive ways to phrase comments so parents can accept what the protégé is saying. "He is working on . . ." or "He is trying to . . ." helps a parent understand a difficult problem a child

NOVEMBER CONFERENCE NOTES

Child's name: _____	
Present at conference: _____	
Date: _____	

Adjustment to _____ grade	Math
Reading	Social Growth/Peer Interaction
Writing	Friends Favorite Choice
Special Service Art, Gym, Computer, Music	Follow-up

Figure 6.2: Form for planning conference notes

may be facing. "Laura enjoys her friends, they like her, and she is trying to learn the appropriate times for socializing and for work. We have developed a special signaling system to help her remember." (See the section on report cards in this chapter for helpful phrases to use.) Protégés should avoid the trap of comparing children and, if parents engage in conversation that invites comparisons, be ready to say that this is not an appropriate topic for discussion.

It is important for protégés to have student work to share. Work from all curriculum areas provides evidence and specific details for the discussion. A good strategy is to have math and science materials available to talk about at the conference. These props help a protégé remember what she wants to say and help parents learn about unfamiliar materials. Conferences are a perfect time to remove the mystery from the language we use and bring parents into the loop. For example, what is "status-of-the-class" and "share" in writing workshop and what are "pattern blocks"?

The Schedule

When I talk with protégés about conferences, the scheduling is an important topic. Protégés might want to carefully construct the schedule so that problem parents, or talkative ones, are in the middle of an afternoon or evening. This helps a protégé keep the conference to a manageable amount of time because another appointment follows. It is tempting to continue a productive or pleasant conversation with a parent and not move along to the next one, but I counsel protégés to keep their appointments (unlike a doctor I know who may keep me waiting for an hour). I suggest that protégés put chairs and books in the hall so that while they wait, parents can sit down and look at what students are reading.

Student Conferences

Protégés may wish to confer with students before they meet with their parents. This dress rehearsal helps the protégé while at the same time it relieves some of the child's concerns. The protégé has the chance to inquire if there was anything the child wants her to share. I know some teachers like to have students attend conferences, but this is not something I recommend to a beginning teacher. Protégés need practice conferring with parents before they try student-attended or student-led conferences.

REPORT CARDS

Reports cards can be a problem when they don't reflect the type of teaching in the classroom. Protégés may teach reading and writing workshop and set rubrics with students and yet have to write a report card that is a mismatch. Sometimes extra comments attached on a separate piece of paper can help to fill this pothole so that student, teacher, and parents will not feel such a large gap between teaching and the report card grades. It is a way for protégés to use their kidwatching skills and report more detail about a student's functioning in the workshop classroom.

Record Keeping

Throughout the fall, as preparation for report card writing, protégés need to keep careful records about each student. This will help them write insightful comments grounded in evidence they have gathered. Assessment of students should take place over time, and it is as dangerous as driving on black ice to rely on memory alone.

The Language of Report Cards

What we put in writing is frozen on the paper, and our words can come back to haunt us. It is helpful to protégés when someone reads their comments for phrasing that is not smooth or is too strong. Also, it is helpful to protégés if someone looks over the grades for inconsistencies. Here is one of my handouts that has words and phrases that may help:

Descriptive words and phrases: is not yet ready to . . . ; shows strength, enthusiasm, enjoyment; exhibits interest in . . . ; wide range of knowledge . . . ; still shows great effort when . . . ; eager, thoughtful, cooperative, age appropriate; contributes eagerly, reluctantly, tentatively; not always available for learning because . . .

Work habits: task commitment, persists, methodical, self-motivated, needs reinforcement, needs reminders, needs structure and monitoring, needs monitoring and rewards

Reading: fluency, comprehension, ability to decode new words, uses context clues, summarizes, interprets, infers, reads widely from a variety of genre

Writing: characteristic voice, uses ideas from reading, range of topic choice and genre, uses dialogue, descriptive language, increasingly elaborated, natural speller

Math: number sense, mental math, problem solving, computation skills, routine applications

Group work: listens, actively listens, works cooperatively with small group, leadership, creative and caring solutions to group problems, contributes to class discussions (eagerly, reluctantly), sense of humor, self-control, part of the classroom community
   Another handout has phrases such as:

- deliberates before acting, tolerates different viewpoints, worries often, takes initiative, exhibits ability, controls emotional outbursts, disciplines himself, dominates the group

- grasps new ideas readily, opens his mind to new ideas, organizes material well, expresses thoughts freely, shows respect for property, thinks critically, welcomes suggestions

If it seems appropriate, I make copies of some of my old report cards and give them to the protégé. We read and discuss them as the protégé begins to write his own comments.

Student Conferences

As with parent conferences, it is a good idea for protégés to take time to show students their report cards before they are sent home. This helps children understand their teacher's thinking, and there are no unpleasant surprises in store. A conference may bear fruit when teacher and child discuss an area that the child needs to attend to during the balance of the school year.

REHEARSING STUDENTS
TO TALK WITH PARENTS

Parents often complain that they do not know what is going on in school, that their children don't discuss the school day with any substance. They want more than a playground report. I teach protégés a strategy to help children talk about school when they get home.

At the end of the day, children gather in a circle to review one aspect of the school day. The protégé asks a question, such as, "What was the most important thing you did with your writing this morning?" Each member of the class responds in turn, going around the circle as students say in their own words what they thought was significant about writing workshop. Other examples of circle questions are:

- What book did you read during independent reading? Would you recommend it to a friend? Why?
- What question did you discuss in your reading response group?
- What did you notice about how your author began the chapter you read today? Did it pull you in?
- What new strategy did you try in your writing today?
- What are you writing now? What are your plans for this piece?

Protégés might tell students the question at the beginning of the day, so they can consider it while they work. Answers are more specific and detailed when the question is carefully framed. Questions need to vary from day to day or they become so routine that responses get sloppy. This review can help students focus their thoughts for an afternoon or dinnertime conversation. When parents ask, "What happened in school today?" the global nature of the question may prevent a child from thinking about one or two important things to share. Of course, another strategy is to help parents ask more specific questions. Guidance about this could be included in a newsletter or special note sent home.

READING RESPONSE JOURNAL

A reading response journal can be organized by the protégé for the parent and child to use at home. This journal should be voluntary for the family. The protégé can send a letter home asking who would like to participate in this activity. The letter explains that the child chooses a book to read with a parent. The parent or the child may read aloud, or they may share the reading. After reading, each person writes a response in the journal. The protégé adds a response when the journal is returned to school—making it a three-way conversation.

Protégés can make these response journals by stapling a dozen pages together with an oaktag cover. Inside the front cover is a list of possible ways to respond to reading, such as:

- I like this book because. . . .
- I recommend this book because. . . .
- My favorite character is, and why. . . .
- This book reminds me of. . . .
- I like the way the author began this chapter because. . . .
- Here are some special sentences I really like. . . .

Reading response journals encourage parent and child to share literature as they help parents understand the kind of reading response and discussion that is occurring in the classroom. How often and how long these journals are used is the decision of the child, the parent, and the protégé.

HELP IN THE CLASSROOM

Protégés have a variety of reactions to parents who want to work in their child's classroom. There are parents who are able to come to school to help even though many homes have two working parents or a single parent who is working. Parents can be extremely helpful in the classroom, especially in the primary grades. Training parents helps them become familiar with the teacher's expectations. Protégés will find it worthwhile to take time to explain their goals for writing workshop, for example, when parents come to school to help students write or publish. My notebook:

> Today in Lesa Tischler's kindergarten classroom two parents sit with their children during the mini-lesson. When children begin to work on their writing, these parents go to different tables in the room. Because kindergarten students need a lot of help with writing, parents are a welcome addition to the classroom.

Parents can help with:

- reading centers
- independent reading
- publishing student writing
- math activities
- science activities
- field trips
- parties and celebrations
- preparation of book club orders

THESE SUGGESTIONS ARE DESIGNED TO HELP STRENGTHEN school/home relationships. They are designed to help protégés as they gain experience working with parents. It is comforting if they have a mentor with whom they can sound out ideas and who will support them as they are initiated into the many forms of parental involvement. I try to help protégés begin the school year with constructive attitudes about how good interaction with parents will assist them in working with children. Each event, Back-to-School Night, conference week, and report card writing is a brand new experience when protégés can use the support of experienced staff. At first, learning a new skill can be tense and time consuming. Once protégés feel comfortable with the parent community, they can slow down the car on the teaching interstate to enjoy the scenery surrounding them.

THE PARENT CONNECTION

- parent letter
- notes
- telephone calls
- newsletters
- back-to-school night
- parent conferences
- report cards
- rehearsing students to talk with parents
- reading response journal
- help in the classroom

7

Stories Speak

When I began to work as a mentor, I assumed that protégés were reading aloud to students and using literature to teach reading and writing skills. Now, I know I cannot take this for granted. Reading aloud needs explicit, extensive discussion and demonstration between mentor and protégé. That is the reason this chapter is included in the book.

"CHILDREN'S BOOKS CAN HAVE MANY PURPOSES, BUT THE most basic one must be to persuade children of something not immediately self-evident, which is that there is a world of stimulation and sensation available through print—that books can carry you out of yourself" (Menand 1997).

Teachers tend to push aside read aloud time when the day becomes busy, as it almost always does. The push for accountability may encourage them to feel that reading aloud is of less value than some other activities. In addition, protégés may be unfamiliar with children's literature or uncertain about how to use read alouds in the service of teaching skills.

In my own classroom, I read aloud at least twice a day. There were two distinct reasons why I took this time. One reason was to introduce read alouds to help me teach reading or writing mini-lessons. The second was to build and strengthen the classroom community. Whether I chose a chapter book to read over a period of time or a picture book, I always selected books I loved and wanted to share. I felt charged with the duty of introducing authors, illustrators, and fine literature to students.

Margaret Moustafa explains that the language of print, of stories, differs from spoken language. In order to become effective readers, children need to understand the language of print. In her book, *Beyond Traditional Phonics, Research Discoveries and Reading Instruction*, Moustafa says, "By ensuring that all children have extensive meaningful experiences hearing stories read to them, schools can help all children learn to understand the language of print as they discover that reading is meaningful" (1997, p. 80).

TIME FOR READING ALOUD

Time is the issue most often raised by protégés as a reason for not reading aloud. We all know that feeling of having too much to do and too little time to do it. Reading aloud can seem like a luxury when the curriculum pressure cooker is ready to blow off steam.

Rituals help to anchor us, so it is helpful when protégés choose a consistent time for the daily reading aloud. A pattern is valuable to the teacher and students. A routine is created for the teacher and the class. If he decides to read aloud every day after lunch, he seems more likely to do it. Students count on the read aloud time and will clamor to hear a book they love. They don't want to miss what happens after Mr. Popper opens the box he has been sent by Admiral Drake in *Mr. Popper's Penguins* (Atwater 1992).

I recommend that protégés consider reading a chapter book without the interruptions that can interfere with enjoyment. It is best to let the tale unfold seamlessly as the author spins her story. This is a time for listening, being wrapped up in language and story. It is worth spending fifteen to twenty minutes of daily class time on this kind of pleasure reading. I counsel protégés to talk about the author's craft and refer back to the chapter book for teaching skills at a later time. A story from my notebook:

> I am in Karen Wrobel's second grade class at Coleytown School to launch the writing workshop. Catherine decides to write about pirates. I am curious about her unusual interest, so I talk with her. "You know, they sail the seven seas," she tells me. Then she looks puzzled. "I don't really know what the seven seas are," but she explains that she heard those words when her mother read to her.

Here is a perfect example of how a young child takes poetic words that are fresh to her and uses them without an exact or clear understanding of their meaning. Catherine is wrapped up in the wonder of language and uses unusual words she's heard as she writes.

Protégés will soon realize how a good book can help everyone settle in for the next activity. Some teachers ask students to listen without doing anything else because they think children will give it more attention. In other classrooms, students may draw during read aloud time. Each protégé needs to work this out his own way.

Whatever time a teacher chooses to read aloud, when the daily schedule is posted in the room (see Chapter 3), read aloud time is an anchor for the day. My notebook:

> Kate Sanderson and I discuss read alouds. This is her fifth year of teaching, and she is committed to reading more often to her class. She has decided that she can open a twenty minute window for reading aloud if she lets go of the daily show and tell. Other days she plans to read aloud while children have their morning snacks. One day after read aloud, children made this list together:

> BOOKS MAKE US RICH:

- rich with learning
- rich with fun
- rich with knowledge
- they stretch our minds
- we go on an imaginary trip

The list certainly verified for Kate why it had been so important to create time in a busy schedule to savor a read aloud.

I try to help protégés envision new ways to tie reading aloud to reading and writing workshop mini-lessons so that time will no longer be a reason for not sharing chapter and picture books. Again, my journal:

> Doris wants to discuss the use of literature for teaching writing skills. She feels she doesn't have time to read a good picture book together with teaching a mini-lesson. It would be too long, and the mini-lesson would be short-changed. I suggest she read the picture book first thing in the morning. Later, she can use the book for the mini-lesson as she focuses on some point in the book that highlights or reinforces her teaching.

A well-crafted book can be plumbed in depth, used again and again for different mini-lessons. When protégés read the book early in the day and then refer to it in detail later, they can provide students the large chunk of time they need for their own reading or writing.

WHY READ ALOUD TO CHILDREN?

Published authors are models for student writers of all ages. One of the best teachers I know is Cynthia Rylant. When I teach a mini-lesson about choosing topics from everyday life, *Henry and Mudge* (1987) is in my hand. If the mini-lesson is about adding detail and using unusual language to provide a picture in the reader's mind, *The Relatives Came* (1985) is a concrete demonstration. If I want to emphasize a sense of place, I use *Night in the Country* (1986). Book discussions and writing improve when students become immersed in the magic of an accomplished writer. A story from my notebook:

> · Whitney McCarthy and I meet one afternoon following her day at summer school. She says something happened in her first grade classroom, but she is not sure what it was. At the end of the year, when she held up a book, the kids understood that they were going to have a discussion, they had things to say, they got excited. In contrast, the summer school students maintain a silence when she holds up a book. They don't have strategies to call upon or the knowledge of how to talk about a book or an author.

Whitney had discovered the importance of the modeling we do as we teach students how to respond to literature, modeling that helps them as readers and writers. In Chapter 3, I described Courtney who was reading *Little House in the Big Woods* (Wilder 1953). Courtney had been inspired to read the book on her own after she heard her teacher read it aloud.

Read alouds signal students that they are part of a shared culture. When I was teaching second grade, I learned that students only knew the movie version of *The Wonderful Wizard of Oz* (Baum 1987). They didn't realize it was a book published almost one hundred years ago.

Lucy Calkins says, "If we are going to design writing workshops in which there are places not only for editing conferences and response groups but also for miracles, we need to bring powerful literature into those classrooms and to do everything possible to invite children to live and write inside that literature. It begins, I think, with believing that the books we read aloud will change everything in the classroom community. And they do. When our children pull close around a shared text, when we read until our eyes shine with tears and we are silenced in the presence of the deepest parts of our lives, it shakes the ground that we and our students stand on as writers and as people" (1994, p. 252).

Literature can model how characters act to solve problems that could occur in our lives. Literature can become a teacher of the moral dilemmas humans face as students discuss the issues presented in stories. My journal:

> Sharon is reading *Stay Away from Simon,* by Carol Carrick (1985) to second graders. They have a heated discussion about whether Josiah and Lucy should have gone with Simon in the snowstorm. Students talk about how

children in the school should treat Simon, a mentally retarded boy. They show their interest, emotions, and reasoning during discussions as they grapple with the compelling issues presented by this book.

WHAT TO READ ALOUD?

Protégés may ask for help with choices for read alouds if they have not had the opportunity to learn much about children's literature. I recommend they take a look at the comprehensive book *Children's Literature in the Elementary School* (Huck, Hepler, and Hickman 1989). It is filled with suggested titles and good ideas.

I like the idea of reading chapter books that introduce students to new authors and themes. The purpose of reading chapter books is enjoyment and building community, but it is possible to choose books that have more impact on classroom life. At the beginning of the year in second grade, I may have read Barbara Dillon's *Good Guy Club* (1980) to help the children become a cohesive social group. There are other books that tie into social studies. Or, books may be chosen simply because they are a good read—they have rich fantasy, powerful language, or are just plain funny. Books enjoyed together help to create the culture of the classroom.

In Chapter 1, I discussed how I selected picture books for the mini-lessons in Millie's fifth grade. In second grade, my choices for picture books varied. When students needed to consider issues of friendship, I chose *George and Martha* (Marshall 1972). If I heard them teasing a peer about something that could not be changed, I would read and provide discussion time for *Chrysanthemum* (Henkes 1991). When the class was doing an author study, it was natural to read a book by that author. If the class was going on a field trip, I looked for an appropriate book. Because time is always an issue, killing two birds with one stone helps take the pressure off.

Following are a few favorite picture books I use for teaching skills. My focus may be on topic choice, story structure, adding details, avoiding repetitive language, using unusual language, creating a sense of place, or devising a problem and finding a solution to it. Readers may wish to look at other books written by these authors.

- *Amelia's Notebook* (Moss 1995)
  Amelia uses her notebook to express her feelings about moving. This book is helpful to teach the concept of keeping a writer's notebook. First, the whole book can be read, then used later, to focus on its parts.
- *Amber on the Mountain* (Johnston 1994)
  A lonely girl meets another child who inspires her to learn how to read

and later, by herself, to write. This book speaks about the value of
friendship and about persistence.

- *Bony-Legs* (Cole 1983)
  A traditional tale; fun to read aloud and for dramatization.

- *Grandfather's Journey* (Say 1993)
  This is a story of a grandfather's journey to America and his feelings of
  love for both Japan and America. This book is useful for topic choice
  in classes where immigrant children are students.

- *I Want a Dog* (Khalsa 1987)
  In this story, a young girl finds ingenious ways to try and convince
  her reluctant parents to get a dog. It teaches about humor in
  writing.

- *Knots on a Counting Rope* (Martin and Archambault 1987)
  A grandfather and his blind grandson reminisce about the boy's birth,
  his first horse, and an exciting horse race. Family stories are good topics for writing. Consider focusing on language and on beautiful illustrations for mini-lessons.

- *Miss Rumphius* (Cooney 1985)
  This book is about a woman who left the world a better place than
  when she was born. Mini-lessons can focus on detail and telling a story
  in the third person, as well as the social message.

- *Miz Berlin Walks* (Yolen 1997)
  The tale of an old lady who tells her stories to a young neighbor. This
  is a multicultural, intergenerational story.

- *Night on Neighborhood Street* (Greenfield 1991)
  This book of poems that explore the sounds, sights, and emotions
  during an evening. Consider mini-lessons about using the senses in
  writing.

- *Nocturne* (Yolen 1997)
  A goodnight story that is pure poetry. This book lends itself to choral
  reading with its magical language.

- *Now One Foot, Now the Other* (de Paola 1980)
  Bobby, the grandson, helps his grandfather Bob recover from a stroke.
  This book is about love and family traditions.

- *Officer Buckle and Gloria* (Rathman 1995)
  When Officer Buckle talks to school children about safety, Gloria, his
  dog, steals the show. This is a humorous story about a dog.

- *Owl Moon* (Yolen 1987)
  Searching for the Great Horned Owl on a snowy night. This Caldecott winner is a book of wondrous language in a quiet mood.

- *Pink and Say* (Polacco 1994)
  Two soldiers from the different armies of the Civil War meet and become friends. This book can teach about the unexpected but human things that can happen.

- *The Relatives Came* (Rylant 1985)
  The house expands with warmth and love when relatives visit. Opportunities for mini-lessons are numerous, including story structure, use of language, detail, and warm, fuzzy feelings.

- *The Snowy Day* (Keats 1962)
  This book is about a young boy's experiences on a snowy day in the city. Keats shows us how to write about the small things children enjoy doing.

- *Spinky Sulks* (Steig 1988)
  Spinky is mad at his family. This is the story of what they do to get him to stop sulking. Humor and the use of adjectives add to this story.

- *Tar Beach* (Ringgold 1991)
  A young girl imagines flying above her Harlem home. Mini-lessons can include the difference between fact and fantasy, how illustration contributes to the story, and the use of language.

I hope protégés will choose to read aloud books they truly love. I strongly recommend becoming familiar with the book and then decide if it is worthwhile before devoting reading time to it. My notebook, again:

> Tracie DeLawrence and I discuss read alouds before school begins. She is planning to read *In the Year of the Boar and Jackie Robinson* (Lord 1984). She taught this book last year during her student teaching and is familiar with it. I applaud her decision to return to a familiar friend the first weeks of her teaching experience.

Reading should be suspended if the class is not enthusiastic about a book. We were taught to feel that we must finish every book we start, but it is good to model that we can abandon a book we don't like. There are too many wonderful books for us to spend time on one that doesn't grab listeners. This story from my notebook is not meant as a criticism of the book, it just didn't work well with this group of young children. The book selection was probably the problem.

Michelle is reading *Stuart Little* (White 1945) to her first grade class. They don't seem to care if she reads or not. She asks me what to do. I give her reasons why she can stop, and I suggest she ask students for their opinions about *Stuart Little*. When the class votes, they decide to choose a different read aloud.

Here is an annotated list of some of my favorite chapter books to read aloud:

- *Babe: The Gallant Pig* (King-Smith 1985)
  Many children have probably seen the movie, but the original book version of the sheep pig is even better.

- *Bridge to Terabithia* (Paterson 1979)
  This book deals with many emotions and issues: school, peers, friendship, death, guilt, and family. It is beautifully crafted.

- *Charlotte's Web* (White 1952)
  All of us love the amazing Charlotte who works to save the life of Wilbur, the pig.

- *Fantastic Mr. Fox* (Dahl 1988)
  This is an outrageous story in the way Roald Dahl can be. Students appreciate the raw humor of this book.

- *I'll Meet You at the Cucumbers* (Moore 1988)
  Moore tells a tale of a country mouse and a city mouse. Tender, amusing story that can be used together with *Adam Mouse's Book of Poems* (Moore 1992).

- *The Indian in the Cupboard* (Banks 1980)
  A toy Indian comes to life and befriends a nine-year-old boy who must feed and protect him. I like the book version much better than the movie.

- *Letters from Rifka* (Hesse 1993)
  This is a moving chronicle of a Jewish family's flight from Russia in 1919 told through the letters of a young girl.

- *Lily's Crossing* (Giff 1997)
  A sensitively written book that is a good vehicle to encourage discussion of World War II issues.

- *The Lion, the Witch, and the Wardrobe* (C. S. Lewis 1995)
  The story of four children who find their way through a wardrobe into the land of Narnia and have exciting adventures.

- *Little House in the Big Woods* (Wilder 1953)
  This story is fascinating to children because of the way people lived on

the frontier. I like it because of the loving, yet real relationships of the family members.

- *The Mouse and the Motorcycle* (Cleary 1990)
  Students love this imaginary story of Ralph who meets a boy and learns about the thrills of motorcycle riding. This is one of three books about Ralph.
- *Mrs. Frisby and the Rats of NIMH* (O'Brien 1971)
  A group of rats become super-intelligent through a series of laboratory injections.
- *My Father's Dragon* (Gannett 1987)
  This is the first book in a series of three and is an excellent fantasy to share with younger students.
- *Walk Two Moons* (Creech 1994)
  A young girl discovers her mother's life and death through a journey with her grandparents.
- *Where the Red Fern Grows* (Rawls 1974)
  A ten-year-old boy trains two hound dogs into top-notch hunting dogs. This story contains both joy and sadness.
- *Winnie-The-Pooh* (Milne 1955)
  If read dramatically, the humor in this book is delightful for both students and reader.

Two books I have used extensively that don't fit into either the picture book or chapter book category are Cynthia Rylant's *Every Living Thing* (1985) and Sandra Cisneros' *The House on Mango Street* (1984). Rylant's book of short stories focuses on the relationships between people and animals and can be examined for the unexpected solutions, language choice, detail, and a myriad of crafting techniques. Cisneros' short, telling vignettes focus on the examination of the small but important things in life. There are pieces about family relationships, feelings, and individual characteristics that resonate with students and move them to write about the details of their own lives.

In *The Read-Aloud Handbook,* Jim Trelease writes that, ". . . of the two forms of literature (fiction and nonfiction), the one that brings us closest and presents the meaning of life most clearly to the child is fiction." He adds, "Reading aloud to children stimulates their interest, their emotional development, and their imagination. . . . Because good literature is precise, intelligent, colorful, sensitive, and rich in meaning, it offers the child his best hope of expressing what he feels" (1984, pp. 27–28).

POETRY

We need to wrap our readers and writers in the wonder of poetry. I was lucky enough to attend a workshop at the International Reading Association with some of the major children's poets of our day: Lee Bennett Hopkins, X. J. Kennedy, Karla Kuskin, and Charlotte Zolotow. In Myra Cohn Livingston's keynote speech, she urged teachers to think of poetry as something to live with daily, stressing that it should not be only a unit taught for three weeks during the year.

As I begin my work with protégés, I find out how familiar they are with children's poetry. Exposure to poetry encourages budding poets to try their hand at writing this genre and to use poetic words as they write in other genre. I model how to use poetry, including the excitement and joy of choral reading. I may lend my poetry books to get teachers started. They contain poems that fit many needs including rhyming and non-rhyming poems. Some of these books are:

- *all the small poems and fourteen more* (Worth 1996)
- *Animal Crackers* (Dyer 1996)
- *Cat Poems* (Livingston 1987)
- *Celebrate America in Poetry and Art* (Panzer, ed. 1994)
- *Eric Carle's Animals Animals* (Carle 1989)
- *Honey, I Love* (Greenfield 1995)
- *The Random House Book of Poetry for Children* (Prelutsky 1983)
- *Reflections on a Gift of Watermelon Pickle . . . and other modern verse* (Dunning, Lueders, and Smith 1967)
- *Sing a Song of Popcorn* (de Regniers, Moore, White, and Carr 1988)
- *Spin a Soft Black Song* (Giovanni 1985)
- *You Be Good & I'll Be Night* (Merriam 1988)

COLLECTING BOOKS
FOR THE CLASSROOM

It is easy for me to assemble a good collection of classroom books because my public library has such a extensive collection. I use the library to gather books for new Westport teachers and to support my work with The Reading and Writing Project. The children's librarians make excellent recommendations, have lists of their favorites at different grade levels, and distribute lists of Newbery and Caldecott winners. Every Westport teacher can have a special sticker on her library card that entitles her to a two-month loan privilege. Another way to collect books is from a commercial book club. When students order books, teachers receive dividends. A careful choice of dividend books can enrich and diversify the classroom library.

Sometimes I see obvious solutions to problems. In the office of a reading teacher in New York City, there is a large collection of picture books. This teacher pulls from the collection for her own work. The school has a poor library, and it seemed as though the books in the reading teacher's office could have heavier traffic if they were available to classroom teachers. I spoke with the reading teacher first and then recommended to protégés that they ask to borrow these books. The reading teacher willingly set up a loan system and the books began to circulate to everyone's satisfaction. Finding a simple solution like this that makes teachers' lives easier is one of the more gratifying aspects of being a mentor.

ORGANIZING THE CLASSROOM LIBRARY

In Chapter 3, I referred briefly to the organization of the classrooom library. Children of all ages can participate in arranging books, which motivates them to keep the library in good shape. I have helped protégés follow a model I used in second grade. I had baskets for books. Early in the school year my students and I spread out the books and looked them over. We established categories: easy-to-read, fairytales, poetry, animal stories, books by Patricia Reilly Giff. That part was easy—we put those books in baskets. Then we discussed other categories we could make. The discussion helped students realize what they knew and needed to know about the books. We talked about how to learn more about unfamiliar books. Categorization took days but stimulated productive reading talk that continued when children wanted to make changes in the groupings later in the year. Donna Skolnick adopted an additional strategy to keep the books in order. Fairytales had a red strip of construction paper put in them and books by James Marshall had a blue one, for example. This helped children return books to the appropriate basket or bin. It is useful to teach students to put books away with the titles facing in the same direction, so they can flip through to see what is there.

Protégés quickly understand the pivotal role teachers play in featuring books. When I brought new books to the room, I placed them on the chalk rail. I gave a book talk about each title and then replaced them on the rail to read aloud and for children to choose as independent reading material.

From my personal library, I put out some books for student use, some I did not. Each teacher can make decisions about how he wants to handle his own books. Again, my notebook:

> As Mara Schwartz moves into her kindergarten room at Coleytown School, she is delighted to see that there are lots of cabinets on the wall, high above where students can reach. She carefully puts away her own books arranged the way she wants them so that she can easily find a title. She knows it would be overwhelming to put too many books out in the beginning of the year. She plans to put out some of these books later and keep some in reserve for her own use.

CHOOSING FAVORITES

I like to model for protégés an activity I used in my classroom. We called it Book-of-the-Week. On Friday, I placed a list of the titles I had read aloud that week on the chalkboard. When we had finished a chapter book, it was on the list. Each child received a piece of scrap paper and wrote down the title of her favorite book for the week. Then, two children helped with the voting. One announced the titles written on the papers, and the other tallied the vote on the chalkboard. Tension rose as we got near the end of the ballots. After the Book-of-the-Week was chosen, its name was entered on a cumulative list hanging in the room. In late May or early June we chose a Book-of-the-Year and reread it. I planned sufficient time for rereading a longer book because the Book-of-the-Year was often a chapter book that had provided deeper discussion and was enjoyed over a longer period of time. Everyone enjoyed revisiting and listening again to the old friend.

"SEEING ADULTS READING WITH ENJOYMENT INCREASES THE chances that children will become lifelong readers" (Kimmel and Segel, p. 22). The purpose for including this chapter in a book about mentor-protégé relationships is to emphasize the importance of reading to children. I have visited many classrooms where reading aloud was not part of the daily routine. I hope both mentors and protégés will reconsider this activity as a must for the daily schedule. We should devote ourselves to sharing fine literature as we use our favorite authors to support the teaching of skills.

BENEFITS FROM READING ALOUD

- to experience the pleasure of listening to a good book
- to use literature as a teacher of skills
- to view problems in literature as models for life
- to understand how literature can be a model for writing
- to encourage and secure an interest in the language of print and in reading
- to promote and receive a shared literary culture
- to observe the pleasure that a joyfully literate adult receives from reading

REFERENCES

Atwater, Richard. 1992. *Mr. Popper's Penguins*. New York: Dell.

Banks, Lynne Reid. 1980. *The Indian in the Cupboard*. Garden City, New York: Doubleday.

Baum, L. Frank. 1987. *The Wonderful Wizard of Oz*. New York: William Morrow.

Calkins, Lucy McCormick. 1994. *The Art of Teaching Writing*. Portsmouth, NH: Heinemann.

Carle, Eric. 1989. *Eric Carle's Animals Animals*. New York: Scholastic.

Carrick, Carol. 1985. *Stay Away from Simon*. New York: Clarion Books.

Cisneros, Sandra. 1984. *The House on Mango Street*. New York: Vintage Books.

Cleary, Beverly. 1990. *The Mouse and the Motorcycle*. New York: Avon.

Cole, Joanna. 1983. *Bony-Legs*. New York: Four Winds Press.

Cooney, Barbara. 1985. *Miss Rumphius*. New York: Puffin Books.

Creech, Sharon. 1994. *Walk Two Moons*. New York: HarperCollins.

Dahl, Roald. 1988. *Fantastic Mr. Fox*. New York: Puffin Books.

de Paola, Tomie. 1980. *Now One Foot, Now the Other*. New York: Putnam.

de Regniers, Beatrice Schenk, Eva Moore, Mary Michaels White, and Jan Carr eds. 1988. *Sing a Song of Popcorn*. New York: Scholastic.

Dillon, Barbara. 1980. *Good Guy Club*. New York: Bantam Books.

Dunning, Stephen, Edward Lueders, and High Smith eds. 1967. *Reflections on a Gift of Watermelon Pickle . . . and other modern verse*. New York: Lothrop, Lee & Shepard.

Dyer, Jane. 1996. *Animal Crackers*. Boston: Little Brown.

Gannett, Ruth S. 1987. *My Father's Dragon*. New York: Knopf

Giff, Patricia Reilly. 1997. *Lily's Crossing*. New York: Delacorte Press.

Giovanni, Nikki. 1985. *Spin a Soft Black Song*. New York: Farrar, Straus and Giroux.

Greenfield, Eloise. 1995. *Honey, I Love*. New York: Harper Festival.

———. 1991. *Night on Neighborhood Street*. New York: Dial Books for Young Readers.

Henkes, Kevin. 1991. *Chrysanthemum*. New York: Greenwillow.

Hesse, Karen. 1993. *Letters from Rifka*. New York: Puffin Books.

Huck, Charlotte S., Susan Hepler and Janet Hickman. 1989. *Children's Literature in the Elementary School*. Fifth Edition. Madison, WI: Brown and Benchmark.

Johnston, Tony. 1994. *Amber on the Mountain*. New York: Dial Books for Young Readers.

Keats, Ezra Jack. 1962. *The Snowy Day.* New York: Viking Press.

Khalsa, Dayal Kaur. 1987. *I Want a Dog.* New York: C. N. Potter.

Kimmel, Margaret Mary and Segel, Elizabeth. 1988. *For Reading Out Loud!* New York: Delacorte Press.

King-Smith, Dick. 1985. *Babe: The Gallant Pig.* New York: Crown.

Lewis, C.S. 1995. *The Lion, the Witch, and the Wardrobe.* New York: HarperCollins.

Livingston, Myra Cohn. 1987. *Cat Poems.* New York: Holiday House.

Lord, Bette Bao. 1984. *In the Year of the Boar and Jackie Robinson.* New York: HarperCollins.

Marshall, James. 1972. *George and Martha.* Boston: Houghton Mifflin.

Martin, Jr., Bill and Archambault, John. 1987. *Knots on a Counting Rope.* New York: Henry Holt.

Menand, Louis. 1997. *The New Yorker.* (October 6): 118.

Merriam, Eve. 1988. *You Be Good & I'll Be Night.* New York: Morrow Junior Books.

Milne, A. A. 1955. *Winnie-The-Pooh.* New York: E. P. Dutton.

Moore, Lilian. 1992. *Adam Mouse's Book of Poems.* New York: Atheneum.

———. 1988. *I'll Meet You at the Cucumbers.* New York: Atheneum.

Moss, Marissa. 1995. *Amelia's Notebook.* Berkeley, CA: Tricycle Press.

Moustafa, Margaret. 1997. *Beyond Traditional Phonics, Research Discoveries and Reading Instruction.* Portsmouth, NH: Heinemann.

O'Brien, Robert C. 1971. *Mrs. Frisby and the Rats of NIMH.* New York: Atheneum.

Panzer, Nora, ed. 1994. *Celebrate America in Poetry and Art.* New York: Hyperion Books for Children.

Paterson, Katherine. 1979. *Bridge to Terabithia.* New York: Avon.

Polacco, Patricia. 1994. *Pink and Say.* New York: Philomel Books.

Prelutsky, Jack, ed. 1983. *The Random Book of Poetry for Children.* New York: Random House.

Rathman, Peggy. 1995. *Officer Buckle and Gloria.* New York: Scholastic, Inc.

Rawls, Wilson. 1974. *Where the Red Fern Grows.* New York: Bantam Books.

Ringgold, Faith. 1991. *Tar Beach.* New York: Crown Publishers.

Rylant, Cynthia. 1985. *Every Living Thing.* New York: Bradbury Press.

———. 1987. *Henry and Mudge, the first book of their adventures.* New York: Bradbury Press.

———. 1986. *Night in the Country.* New York: Bradbury Press.

———. 1985. *The Relatives Came.* New York: Bradbury Press.

Say, Allen. 1993. *Grandfather's Journey.* Boston: Houghton Mifflin.

Steig, William. 1988. *Spinky Sulks.* New York: Farrar, Straus and Giroux.

Trelease, Jim. 1984. *The Read-Aloud Handbook.* New York: Penguin Books.

White, E. B. 1952. *Charlotte's Web.* New York: Harper & Row.

———. 1945. *Stuart Little.* New York: Harper & Row.

Wilder, Laura Ingalls. 1953. *Little House in the Big Woods.* New York: Harper & Row.

Worth, Valerie. 1996. *all the small poems and fourteen more.* New York: Farrar, Straus and Giroux.

Yolen, Jane. 1997. *Miz Berlin Walks.* New York: Philomel Books.

———. 1997. *Nocturne.* New York: Harcourt Brace.

———. 1987. *Owl Moon.* New York: Philomel Books.

8

Peer Coaching

ANOTHER MODEL FOR GROWTH

I began teaching in September 1967. That school year, and the succeeding twenty-two, I participated in the standard evaluation procedure used in Westport. A succession of administrators, with yellow or white pads in hand, dropped in to view my teaching while they sat quietly and made notes. Later, I was given an appointment to talk about that observation essentially to hear their view of one lesson on one day in a continuum of lessons and days. There was no pre-observation conference, and the visit was unannounced. These observations seemed to have little connection with a goal-setting process used by the district. For that, I was asked to meet with my principal and set a professional goal each September. How and when I worked on that goal was left to my discretion.

IN 1988, WESTPORT STAFF RECEIVED A MEMO FROM THE teachers in charge of a new peer coaching program stating that "teachers may engage in goal-setting/attainment activities by electing to participate in peer coaching." Those who decided to join this group would step aside from the regular evaluation process. Teachers who volunteered were free to choose partners with whom they wanted to work. The memo further stated that "Participants will be expected to take part in training, goal-setting, and will observe and conference with colleagues."

This letter asked us why we would elect the peer coaching process. "Are you interested in talking with teachers about teaching? Would you benefit from specific feedback from a colleague? Have you been looking for an opportunity to observe colleagues at work? The peer coaching process reduces feelings of isolation often experienced by teachers. Participants will help shape the process to meet district and individual needs. This is an opportunity to collaborate with colleagues and engage in professional development directly related to personal goals."

An article in *Educational Leadership*, "Cooperative Professional Development: Peer-Centered Options for Teacher Growth" describes five major functions of peer coaching identified by Beverly Showers (Glatthorn 1987, pp. 33–34). I will refer to these five points throughout this chapter. They are:

1. Companionship: teachers talk about their successes and frustrations which reduces their sense of isolation.
2. Teachers provide each other technical feedback as they practice new teaching strategies. The feedback is not evaluative.
3. There is an emphasis on the analysis of new teaching strategies with the goal of internalizing them so that they become spontaneous and flexible, a part of the everyday repertoire.
4. The peer coach helps the teacher adapt her teaching to the specific needs of particular students and helps the teacher analyze student responses and modify the strategy as needed.
5. The coach provides support that facilitates trials of new strategies.

Milbrey Wallin McLaughlin and Sylvia Mei-ling Yee in "School as a Place to Have a Career," an article in *Building A Professional Culture in Schools,* (Lieberman 1988, p. 31) report results from a survey of teachers about the importance of different items that support improved teaching. Forty-eight percent of those surveyed ranked "more time for reflection on teaching practices or planning with colleagues" at or near the top.

When we received the information about peer coaching, my friend and colleague, Caltha Crowe, and I were both feeling the need for time to reflect and plan, and we liked the idea of planning together toward improving our professional strategies. I was teaching second grade and Caltha was teaching fourth grade at Coleytown School. We welcomed the prospect of having the opportunity to see each other and talk about the specifics of teaching. We felt it would help us grow if we could work together to develop our kidwatching skills together and discuss how we taught struggling readers.

We decided to join the local peer coaching program. Our friendship played an important role in this decision. Caltha and I met when she came to Westport as an experienced teacher. At that time, we learned that we had many similar interests and were in general agreement on philosophical attitudes toward teaching and learning. We discovered that we worked well together when we planned and taught a series of inservice workshops on reading for new Westport teachers.

In this chapter, I will describe a small part of our peer coaching work that began in October 1989 and continued for three years. The district provided a leader who arranged and conducted sessions for participating teachers on professional days. Our training included background information about the theory of peer coaching and instruction about how partners or groups could work together. We looked at methods of data collection, conferring, and observation techniques. We examined the Connecticut Competency Instrument that had been developed by our state for teachers and administrators to evaluate beginning teachers. As the professional days continued through the first and second years, peer coaches shared their experiences with the whole group. In addition, different models of working together were discussed.

The professional days provided us with the opportunity to talk and plan with our peer partners. Caltha and I were eager for time to plan our work together, an activity that resulted in a decrease in our sense of isolation as we shared views of teaching. Both the Westport memo inviting teachers to participate in peer coaching and the Glatthorn article mentioned peer coaching as a way of conquering the sense of isolation. This was certainly evident as we discovered what we wanted to do and ways we wanted to help each other. The peer coaching program was tailor-made for teachers like us.

The history of our working together centered around reading. It began in Caltha's fourth grade classroom when I was a district staff developer and she was a new teacher in the district. At that time, we focused attention on two areas: reading response groups and nonfiction reading comprehension. In succeeding years, Caltha developed her teaching strategies far beyond those I had introduced in her classroom. When I returned to the classroom, I organized a reading workshop using both oral and written readers' response and taught children how to work in reader response groups. I taught nonfiction reading strategies to the whole class using short articles I had collected for this purpose. It was natural for us to focus attention on the reading area.

FIRST STEPS IN PLANNING

As we talked about our reading workshop classes, we began to look for areas where we could help each other. As identified by Beverly Showers, the opportunity for companionship and conversation helped us understand that we both wanted to look at the work of individual students and that we felt our work should be directly related to instruction. We also decided we would establish criteria for measuring our success based upon classroom observation.

We were interested in individual student participation. I wanted to use nonfiction reading lessons as my focus, and Caltha thought about looking at students in reading response groups. We both wanted to zero in on students who had less well-developed reading skills.

I identified Jim as the student in my class to highlight. He had spent an extra year in kindergarten and was not reading as well as one would hope. He seemed reluctant, hesitant, and self-conscious. He was quiet in class as if he didn't want to call attention to himself for fear that the teacher would notice him. Yet, it appeared that he was bright, perhaps smarter than his present reading ability indicated.

Caltha chose Matt. He was new to our school. He wanted to belong to the literacy club, he pretended to be a good reader and chose books that were too difficult for him. Therefore, he was a member of a response group in which other students were reading at a higher level.

SCHEDULING

After each of us identified the individuals we wanted to look at within the context of our reading classes, we talked together about those students. Then we examined our respective schedules to find convenient times when we could visit and work in each other's classroom. We agreed to use our planning time and lunch hour if necessary. This meant some adjustment in the time we taught reading, but we had the luxury to be flexible. Our goal was to plan one visit a week, but we found that sometimes conflicting obligations interfered. We did not crowd our schedules, but tried to be realistic about how much time we could devote to this work. The log we kept indicates that in reality we worked together two, perhaps three times a month. Luckily, no one imposed any expectations on us, they were our own. We were willing to use planning or lunchtime for peer coaching work because we anticipated positive outcomes.

RECORD KEEPING

We knew we should keep records to which we could refer in the future. Documenting our work seemed important, but we needed some way that was clear-cut and relatively quick. We were realistic about elaborate plans that would probably never be realized. We agreed that at the end of each of our meetings one of us would write quick notes in a notebook we would keep together. We shared this responsibility. It was an easy task because we did it together as both of us contributed to the thinking. These notes proved especially useful during our second and third years of peer coaching.

OBSERVATION

We thought that during our initial classroom visits we would script the words of the teacher and the behavior and words of students. But we discovered that scripting was difficult. We simplified the recording by scripting only the teacher talk and that of the child we were observing, Jim or Matt. We did this on a class list. Each time any child talked, we tracked it with a tally mark next to his name. We scripted Matt or Jim in the space after his name. Later we tried a second method using the seating plan, making tallies and drawing lines to show interaction in the class, which gave us additional information. To indicate what we were recording, Caltha observed whole class lessons on comprehension strategies, and I observed the conversation in Matt's reading response group.

We were engaged in the second and third major functions of peer coaching identified by Showers, that of providing technical feedback and analysis of teaching. After each set of visits, we analyzed and discussed what we had done to discover useful information about our roles as teachers and about the individual children we had identified for study. One thing we already knew, of course, was that when a teacher is involved with a whole class of children it is sometimes difficult to focus on individuals and accurately see what is going on. The second set of eyes and the documentation were welcome.

After discussing Caltha's observations in my class, I realized, for example, that I avoided calling on Jim even when he tentatively looked as though he wanted to say something. Perhaps I was reluctant to single him out when he didn't definitely indicate he wanted to talk. In addition, Caltha suggested that I be more explicit about the purposes of the comprehension lesson—why we were doing it. It was certainly clear from the script and from Caltha's observations of Jim that I had identified a student who could benefit from extra help. The question then was, what to do about it? How could we assist him to become a better reader and to participate in the discussion? The possibility of brainstorming about this with a partner was a welcome experience.

VIDEOTAPING

We had a video recorder available, so we decided to try taping to see whether it was more useful than our note taking. The taping was done in two ways. We taped each other, and we each taped students in our own classrooms.

I found the videotaping useful for seeing facial expressions and distracting behaviors that occurred during lessons, but it was limited, of course, to where the camera lens was directed. It was impossible to tape Jim or Matt alone without making them self-conscious. Unlike a person, the video camera has no peripheral vision. When I was taping in my own classroom, I felt I had to ignore much of what was happening in the rest of the room. In addition, the quiet voices of young students were difficult to hear on the tapes. Caltha purchased an extra microphone inexpensively at a local electronics store and put it on a table in the middle of the response group. This helped when we taped the conversation of students around a table, but in my opinion, videotaping had severe limitations for our purposes, not the least of which was the extra time it took to view the tapes.

GOAL SETTING

Early in our work, we decided to use classroom observation to gauge the success of our intervention. Later we realized we wanted to do more than that. We decided to set some goals for teaching the students we identified for study. We wanted to focus on how to improve our skills to attain a better understanding of individual students who needed help. Once we had that deeper grasp, we needed to decide what we could or should do with those understandings over time. Each of us identified students who presented us with puzzles, who we wanted to better know and understand. Each of us identified a student who could benefit from individual help. The scripts confirmed that. We decided to talk over and decide on intervention strategies with these students, use those strategies, and then measure our success and/or failure based upon further observation in each other's classrooms. Our assessment plan included talking both with the students and their parents.

STUDENT INTERVIEWS

To follow the fourth function of peer coaching identified by Showers, adapting the teaching to the needs of particular students, we decided to use student interviews. We would talk with these individuals about their behavior and skills to see whether they recognized a difference before and after our planned intervention. These interviews would help us determine how successful we were with our interventions. The discussion that follows is more focused on my student because I am the writer.

Jim and I talked a long time about his reading. He had a fairly accurate picture of himself as a reader. It was a laborious task for him, something he resisted. Jim stumbled and hesitated because he lacked confidence and had poorly developed skills for tackling unknown words. He failed to predict, in his head, what he thought would come next in the text. He had fallen into bad habits and had a negative attitude toward reading. I talked with him about working on strategies for figuring out words from context and using phonetic clues. I planned to work with the entire class on prediction strategies but to give Jim an individual boost in addition to the group work. When asked if he thought better fluency would help him feel more positive about reading, his answer was a definite yes.

We chose a three-pronged intervention for Jim. First, I went to work helping him with strategies for figuring out new words, using contextual clues combined with better decoding. Second, I talked with him frequently about prediction, trying to build in the habit while he read. We worked from reading material of his choice. I could quickly see an attitude change. This may have come about because he enjoyed having the individual assistance, but it was also clear that Jim was feeling a growing confidence about reading.

The third part of our intervention with Jim involved Caltha's student, Matt. We trained Matt to help Jim. Our thinking was that it would call upon altruistic qualities in Matt in the guise of assisting a second grader while, at the same time, help him with his own reading skills. I showed Caltha how to teach Matt using a strategy called echo reading. Working with him on echo reading so that he could do it with Jim was a face-saving way of improving Matt's reading fluency. We arranged a time and place for the boys to work. We were following Showers' fourth and fifth functions, modifying the model to the specific needs of individual students while the coach helped facilitate the trial of new teaching strategies.

After a number of sessions of echo reading, Jim and Matt began to develop a bond of friendship. Matt would stop in our room to pick up Jim at bus time. When the two classes got together for activities, they liked to sit next to each other. They were not far apart in age because Jim had spent an extra year in kindergarten. And Matt didn't have too many friends yet in his new school. We had not predicted this as an outcome, but working together apparently satisfied mutual needs in these boys.

TEACHER OBSERVATION

Caltha and I could suddenly see a change in Jim's attitude and in his class participation. It was clear that he felt more confident and willing to engage in both small group and whole class reading activities. He was choosing more challenging books for his independent reading. It was a great feeling: the peer coaching work brought about growth in reading for Jim who had presented problems that had been recognized but unresolved throughout his school life.

Interviewing Jim again served to confirm our observations. He expressed his growing confidence about reading by saying that he preferred reading workshop when he read nonfiction. He talked about how he liked to choose his own books and went on to speak about his favorite fiction author, James Stevenson, because he enjoyed the cartoon format of many of Stevenson's books.

With Matt the change was slower. Caltha discussed book choice with him. She talked with me about how to teach him to use context clues and worked with him on fluency. Disguised as a way to continue helping Jim, I did some echo reading with him outside the classroom where his self-esteem would not suffer. After several months, we could see small changes but because he was older, the problems were more entrenched and growth was slower.

PARENTAL OBSERVATION

It seemed natural for parent observation to be our third method for assessment. We decided early in our talks that we were interested in bringing parents into the loop. Our goal was to help them understand more about the reading workshop and give them a clearer view of how their children were doing in school. We planned to begin the discussion about our observations and interventions during the November parent conferences. We would ask for parent input and comments.

Caltha was concerned about talking with Matt's mother. When Caltha first met her she expressed her worries about his reading. We discussed this and decided she could explain our strategy of having Matt help a younger child: that we felt this would provide a comfort and reading level appropriate for Matt at this time. His mother was supportive and relieved that Caltha had found an activity that would help Matt feel less overwhelmed by reading. She was ready to wait and see how this developed.

Early in the school year Jim's mother had expressed anxiety about his reading. He had experienced a slow start in school, including that extra year in kindergarten. When we began our work with Jim, I spoke with her again. We talked in detail so she was aware of how I was working with context and phonetic clues and with prediction. I coached her so she could be consistent and use these techniques informally at home. As Matt prepared to work with Jim, we talked again so I could explain the echo reading.

When interviewed later in the school year, she was eager to report her observation that Jim was more interested in books and in reading at home. His second grade homework, reading fifteen to twenty minutes each evening, was now done willingly and not viewed as a punishment.

STUDENTS AS MENTORS

After the Jim and Matt experience, we thought there might be some benefits from having our two classes share their thinking over carefully posed questions about the reading workshop. We gathered both classes together for periodic discussions. We were startled to observe that younger children could act as role models for older ones, as well as vice versa. An example of this was the discussion about book choice. When Margaret, a fourth grader, said she chose books based on the recommendation of her friends, Mindy, a second grader, followed her by saying that sometimes those recommendations didn't work well and that it was a good idea to read a few pages to check if the book was too easy or too hard. Sharon, a second grader, told everyone in the circle how she liked to read the book flap or the summary on the back before deciding about a book to read. She stated that this helped her know if she would be interested in the book.

REFERRALS

Sometimes our peer coaching work led to referrals within the school to get additional help for a child. I had a student named Nina who presented a puzzle we could not solve. True, we knew that she had suffered through some serious family disruptions. But still we could not figure out why she was not a better reader. Our school had a child study team that made suggestions to teachers on how to modify the environment for individual students. Child study team referrals preceded possible special education referrals. After both of us evaluated Nina and worked with her individually, we decided to refer her to the child study team. Several interesting suggestions resulted from this meeting, but they were not enough to unlock Nina's problem. Later, she was evaluated for special education but did not qualify. At least we tried all the avenues open to us. Succeeding years showed that Nina needed time to develop and mature before she could apply all her native ability to school work.

CALTHA AND I WERE CONTINUOUSLY EVALUATING AND RE-evaluating what we were doing. As Showers pointed out, the opportunity to talk together provided an intense learning experience and helped us expand our teaching repertoires. Each of the three years of our participation in the peer coaching program brought about fine-tuning of our observational and pedagogical skills as well as our ability to work as a team. With practice we were able to help each other even more as we assisted individual students with more entrenched problems. The value of working together seemed evident from the beginning, but increased as we became better at it. The three years could easily have lasted a longer time if I had not retired in June 1992.

From my point-of-view, this work was much more powerful than the previous goal setting and performance review done with an administrator. My commitment to it was stronger, I spent more time reflecting on it, and worked harder at it. The goals were mine to set and revise, plus the excitement of working with a valued colleague far surpassed the many years of working alone trying to resolve questions about individual student behavior or performance.

The strength of our teacher-to-teacher work was the shared goals and flexibility built into the work. We were challenged and excited to learn together. We looked critically at our teaching and our students, as we found fertile ground for study and growth.

PEER COACHING	
Planning	Goal Setting
	Identification of problem
	Identification of students
	Scheduling
	Record keeping
Observation	Scripting
	Videotaping
Intervention	Direct teaching
	Student modeling
	Individual
	Class to class
	Referrals
Evaluation	Student interview
	Teacher observation
	Parent interview

REFERENCES

Glatthorn, Allan A. 1987. "Cooperative Professional Development: Peer-Centered Options for Teacher Growth." *Educational Leadership.* (November): 33–34.

McLaughlin, Milbrey Wallin and Sylvia Mei-ling Yee. 1988. School as a Place to Have a Career. In *Building A Professional Culture in Schools.* Lieberman, Ann, ed. New York: Teachers College Press.

Epilogue

As I look back over my years as a mentor, I recognize five time-tested principles upon which I grounded my work. These are:

- A mentor must be responsive to individual learners, recognizing the learners as individuals with unique needs and interests.
- Flexibility is essential; mentoring work must be tailored to fit the needs and pace of the individual learner.
- Mentoring is grounded in sensitive, skilled observation.
- A close, honest relationship is the foundation of effective mentoring.
- Lifelong learning is a goal of the mentoring relationship.

Each day my schedule and the weather allow, I take a long brisk walk in my neighborhood. I smell wood fires in winter and gaze at gardens in summer. In spring I watch as leaves begin to grow, and in autumn I observe the colors change. Sometimes the wind is at my back, sometimes it ruffles my hair.

The relationship I establish with a protégé can be like the seasons with their changing winds. I may sail along on a lovely smooth spring day. Or I may need to push forward against a cold, damp blowing wind. What makes the conditions so variable is often hard to determine, although one factor may be that people are as different and diverse as the weather.

In the classroom, I sharpened my skills to teach every child, no matter what her learning style, her personality, her level of development, or her skills. When mentors work with protégés, they need to take all these factors into consideration. Each protégé is a unique individual who comes to the learning situation equipped with his own skills, interests, and abilities.

In the classroom, I learned to pace myself according to how fast or how slowly students were learning. When mentors work with protégés, they need to reflect upon how quickly those protégés absorb and begin to use new strategies and skills. It isn't wise to offer so much that a protégé feels as if he were teetering at the edge of a precipice.

In the classroom, I tried to be a careful, deliberate planner who grounded teaching in observation and record keeping. Mentors are most effective when they have long-range goals for expanding teaching repertoires in consonance with the aims and abilities of their protégés.

In the classroom, I learned to do an about face and retrace my steps when it looked as though what I planned was running up against a stone wall. The same is true for teaching adult learners. If it doesn't work because a mentor is too far out in front, or going too quickly, or doesn't present material in a clear manner, then it is wise to backtrack and try again, perhaps in another way.

When I worked with young children, I learned to build strong relationships with them, bonds based upon listening and close observation. When adults work with other adults, the same holds true. Adult learners will absorb much more if we can achieve a relationship that is based on give and take, an honest partnership that includes deep conversations and authentic evaluation.

I really enjoy children; I take pleasure in being with them. I love their thinking and their humor. Part of my job is helping protégés revel in the quirky things that happen and the fun of being with students as each day unfolds.

When I worked with children, my goal was to help them become life-long readers and writers. This goal holds for my work with adults. I hope they will become lifelong learners, if they aren't already. This is achieved partly by making the learning journey exciting enough that protégés will reach beyond the boundaries of their present practices as they diversify and expand their repertoires.

The listening and communication skills I used in the classroom apply to working with adults. It is important to be honest, clear, and concise. The relationship with protégés is not about me, it is about them. I bring to bear all my knowledge about teaching reading and writing together with classroom management strategies, but everything I do is fashioned to fit the individual protégé.

As I walk the path of staff development, I try to use the same skills I use as I walk through my neighborhood: clear vision, acute hearing, delight in the unexpected, and varied pace depending upon the temperature or the wind. Each protégé is a distinct individual who must, in the end, chart her own trail, find her own beauty, hear her own calls, and reach out to what interests and delights her. The wind may increase her speed, or she may need to step around obstacles. My job is to equip protégés with the right gear and knowledge of the terrain so they can strike out on their own and chart new paths to explore. I wish them wonder, success, and joy in their journey of teaching and learning.

Index